Intersections

Manchester University Press

Cinema Aesthetics
Series editors Des O'Rawe and Sam Rohdie

Since the 1970s, many academics and teachers have been taking the study of film out of Film Studies by producing curricula and critical literature hostile to notions of artistic endeavour and aesthetic value. An old heresy is a new orthodoxy, and the argument that the cinema exists solely to illustrate the politics of culture, identity and pleasure is no longer an argument; it is now a 'core doctrine' of film education, particularly in the UK and the US. The Cinema Aesthetics series aims to challenge this orthodoxy by publishing visually literate and intellectually creative studies that explore a specific term, critical category, or interdisciplinary issue.

Also available
Stefania Parigi *Cinema – Italy* (ed. Sam Rohdie and Des O'Rawe; trans. Sam Rohdie)
Steven Peacock *Colour*
Sam Rohdie *Montage*

Intersections
Writings on cinema

Sam Rohdie

Manchester University Press

Copyright © Sam Rohdie 2012

The right of Sam Rohdie to be identified as the author of this work has been asserted by him in accordance with the Copyright, Designs and Patents Act 1988.

Published by Manchester University Press
Altrincham Street, Manchester M1 7JA, UK
www.manchesteruniversitypress.co.uk

British Library Cataloguing-in-Publication Data is available

ISBN 978 0 7190 8692 2 hardback

First published 2012

The publisher has no responsibility for the persistence or accuracy of URLs for any external or third-party internet websites referred to in this book, and does not guarantee that any content on such websites is, or will remain, accurate or appropriate.

Typeset in Scala and Scala Sans display
by Koinonia Ltd, Manchester

Ai miei amici Stefania Parigi e Adriano Aprà per tante belle cose

Contents

Acknowledgements	*page* viii
List of illustrations	ix
Preface	xi
Louis Feuillade	1
Jean Painlevé	5
Jean Vigo	14
Georges Franju	20
Jacques Tati	24
Raymond Depardon	30
Alfred Hitchcock	44
Jacques Rivette	53
Jean-Luc Godard	71
Orson Welles	88
Anthony Mann	105
Luchino Visconti	111
François Truffaut	129
John Ford	135
Bibliography	138

Acknowledgements

I am deeply indebted to Desmond O'Rawe for his support, encouragement, friendship and wit. I always have a sense of his positive presence in any work I do including the preparation of this book.

List of illustrations

1 *Judex*, Louis Feuillade
  Société des Etablissements, L. Gaumont (1916)   *page* 65
2 *Science in fiction, the sea horse*, Jean Painlevé
  Cinégraphie Documentaire (1934)   65
3 *L'Atalante*, Jean Vigo
  Jean-Louis Nounez (1934)   66
4 *L'Atalante*, Jean Vigo.
  Jean-Louis Nounez (1934)   66
5 *Blood of the Beast*, Georges Franju.
  Forces et voix de la France ((1949)   67
6 *Playtime*, Jacques Tati
  Jolly Film, Specta Films (1967)   67
7 *La Vie moderne*, Raymond Depardon
  Palmeraie ed Désert, France 2 Cinema, Arte
  France (co-production) Canal+, Centre National
  de la Cinématographie, Région Ile-de-France
  support) (2008)   67
8 *Vertigo*, Alfred Hitchcock.
  Alfred J. Hitchcock Productions, Paramount
  Pictures (1958)   68
9 *Jeanne la Pucelle I – Les batailles*, Jacques Rivette
  France 3 Cinéma, La Sept Cinéma, Pierre Grise
  Productions (1994)   68
10 *Histoire(s) du cinéma*, Jean-Luc Godard
  (1988–98)   68

11 *F for Fake*, Orson Welles
    Janus Film, SACI (1973) 69
12 *Man of the West*, Anthony Mann
    Ashton Productions Inc (1958) 69
13 *La terra trema*, Luchino Visconti
    Universalia Film, (1948) 69
14 *Shoot the Piano Player*, François Truffaut
    Les Films de la Pléiade, (1960) 70
15 *She Wore a Yellow Ribbon*, John Ford
    Argosy Pictures Corporation (1949) 70

Preface

The essays in this book have been written in specific circumstances and for specific occasions over a period of just a few years. They do not assume the presence of each other nor together do they form a coherent narrative or lead to a conclusion, or demonstrate a thesis. They are not illustrations of a plan. Each is an essay that is tentative, speculative, open, questioning, and each is separate. They should be seen as journeys, or perhaps more exactly as wanderings, and without particular destinations. They have been placed in contact with each other, side by side, like seating of guests for a dinner party, though not exactly. The essays have a tendency to turn back and turn around, move in circles, in short to reposition themselves and, by their encounters, create filiations and associations that otherwise might not occur, in short, surprises. It is this manner of writing (essayist) and this manner of joining (a montage) and this attitude of provocation as a consequence of chance meetings that is at the heart of this book. Ideas are come upon and relations formed rather than predetermined, and nothing secure because subject to change to an instantaneous spark or realisation, when something that had been dormant reappears, is resurrected and new paths and possibilities pointed to though not exactly travelled. It is fitting therefore, perhaps, more unconscious on my part than a matter of design, that the book begins with essays on the Surrealists and that Godard is present everywhere.

Louis Feuillade

Louis Feuillade began scripting films in 1905 after failing to succeed as a writer and then started making films in 1906, not unlike D.W. Griffith who drifted into film from theatre and acting. A year later, in 1907, Feuillade was appointed Artistic Director at Gaumont studios where he worked until 1918. He made about 630 films (he claimed 800) until his death in 1925. Feuillade is most celebrated for his serial films: *Fantômas* (1913–1914), *Le Vampire* (1915) and *Judex* (1916) appreciated by the French Surrealists and Luis Buñuel, Alain Resnais and Georges Franju (who remade his own *Judex* in 1963).

It is difficult to perceive an itinerary in Feuillade's serials either for the characters or for the films. His characters seem to be forever in an unknown realm. Nothing and no one is ever what they appear to be and every path pursued becomes tortuous, like a labyrinth. Accords are within rather than between shots. Connective editing is minimal and depth more important than line, spectacle more emphasised than story or narrative. His films exhibited, like most films of this early period, the presence of the fairground and vaudeville 'attractions', that is, the relation of shots tended to be associative rather than linear, essentially autonomous sequences each with a beginning and an end, not unlike the montage of attractions in Eisenstein's *Battleship Potemkin* (1925).

In *Le Vampire*, there are two parallel worlds, the bourgeois (good) and the criminal (evil). The parallelism is only apparent since the worlds permeate each other and are defined by and dependent upon their contrary. Much of the film concerns infiltrations, impossible apparitions from out of a depth or from the invisible, disguises, false identities, masks, sudden revelations and surprising (and unlikely) occurrences. In Feuillade's universe it is difficult to say with certainty what anything is since nothing is stable, neither identities nor objects are what they seem to be.

It is impossible not to think of Chaplin in this regard where the most ordinary objects are transformed, metamorphosed by Chaplin into something else and with other functions so that the world and all that is in it can become entirely different, an invention, a fantasy. In Chaplin, such transformations were a source of gags and of admiration for Charlie's imagination and of 'Charlie' himself who in his very being is a hodgepodge of identities, multiple directions and associations, tramp and gentleman.

The confusions created by Feuillade, marked by disguise and masks, belong to a theatrical tradition of farce (the *commedia dell'arte*) and of high comedy (Shakespeare, Marivaux, Beaumarchais), and as well to a new 'modern' novelistic and popular genre of detective fiction of the late nineteenth and early twentieth century (Edgar Allan Poe, Conan Doyle, Agatha Christie and, later, Georges Simenon) where there are not simply two worlds (good and evil), but alternative and multiple ones. Hitchcock is heir to that tradition.

Each suspect in the detective story exemplifies different, often opposed possible 'other' narratives, housed by the principal narrative which is a search among alternatives for the correct one. The narrative of detective fiction is a quest for *the* narrative both within and outside it. The task of the detective is to negotiate and journey amid a labyrinth of virtual stories until he finds the 'one' story (the 'true' among multiple fictions) which, once found, allays (resolves, unravels) confusions, false paths, uncertainties, suspicions that constituted the landscape of the detective novel, essentially an internal 'intellectualised' landscape. In such fiction, reason is doubly restored. It is the instrument for uncovering the true that the novel had severely disturbed, deferred, perverted or confused. What is uncovered, however irrational it might be, is explained – that is, rationalised, brought back to reason, everything made whole, certain, normalised once again, identities secured (revealed) above all stabilised, restored to a reasonable world, the impossible made sense of, the unknown explained, the formless defined.

The reason that crime, false identity, masquerade are so disruptive (acts of violence, shock, sudden laughter, the unlikely) is that their presence is ubiquitous. Every boundary, category, idea, person, object in a Feuillade film is porous and at risk. What is told in a Feuillade narrative is that nothing, including the telling of it, is sure as occurs in Resnais' *L'Année dernière à Marienbad* (1961) or the novels of Alain Robbe-Grillet. As with detective fiction, it is less what is narrated that becomes the subject than the process of narration, as if the fiction is a mirror reflecting itself and that it turns into spectacle. All fictions, all images (and language) are unstable, as if instability is a normal state and stability only tentative, a struggle to achieve yet always under threat, which for Godard in his films is a strategy of constant interruptions, divergences, multiple pathways.

Feuillade (without suggesting filiation or influence) was a contemporary of Sigmund Freud, Henri Bergson, Marcel Proust and Franz Kafka, all belonging to the early period of modernism, a time where the idea of the unified personality, hence the unified narrative in which such a personality had been contained and had existed as hero or heroine, as centre and focus, no longer held nor could be relied upon or clearly identified. What you see in Feuillade as in Freud, Kafka and Proust is the disintegration of a former consensus, of a past, which to these writers, is already in ruins. The idea of the 'person' (character, personality) was undermined by the 'unconscious', the irrational, by dreams, reveries, memories, fantasies, metamorphoses, which, however real their base and origin, transformed and transmuted such that confusion, masquerade, false identity, relativity, formlessness, overlapping times, nothingness and divided selves were not exceptions but the norm.

Feuillade's films are voyages, adventures in space and time, and every voyage, as in fairy tales, a labyrinth of obstacles, surprises, encounters and dead ends. With each sequence, with each image and sound, his films seem to be refashioned, beginning again, taking a new path, in flux, getting lost, going astray and as a consequence of the very act of seeking certainties and solidities whereas the only real in Feuillade is the uncertain fuelled by love or by its variant, greed. The journeys that become labyrinthine issue from a world of realities reconfigured to become mysterious and marvellous, shaped by dreams and fears that surface (as in Alfred Hitchcock), where anything can happen, where the world can be remade, everything in it only potential and open, often improbable because now determined by subjectivities as in Hitchcock's *The Birds* (1963).

Jean Painlevé

Jean Painlevé made his first film in 1927 and his last in 1982; in all he made more than 200 films, many now lost. With few exceptions the films were documentary shorts of marine fauna, small marine animals, predominantly crustaceans, whose homes were at the floor of the sea in caves, mud, among algae: shrimp, sea urchins, the seahorse, octopus, sea animals – that is, animals seemingly most distant from humans, most undeniably other and alien, least attended to, written about, documented or mythologised, no Moby Dicks, no sharks, none of the big game fish of Ernest Hemingway and Howard Hawks, in short, at the margins of the animal world and of human culture.

Painlevé wrote the commentary for Georges Franju's *Le Sang des bêtes* (1949). He was sympathetic to Jean Vigo (as was Franju). All three employed French modern music in their films, notably of Maurice Jaubert, also American jazz and collages of fragments of music from classical composers. Painlevé used compositions by Duke Ellington for his *Le Vampire*, a film about bloodsucking bats and their victim, a cuddly hamster.

Painlevé, like Franju, Buñuel and Vigo, was close to French Surrealism, though he would break his ties with André Breton's Surrealism because it seemed too doctrinaire, therefore prescriptive and limiting. And he had a different view of reality to Breton's; for Breton – and it is obvious in Buñuel-Salvador Dalí's *Un Chien andalou* (1929) and *L'Âge d'or* (1930), films that Breton applauded – surreality (reality plus) was dream and fantasy made real, whereas for Painlevé surreality was not the projection of dream onto the everyday, but the discovery of the marvellous in the everyday. Painlevé was more in accord with the poet Ivan Goll, who broke with Breton and 'official' Surrealism for similar reasons. In substance, however, the doctrinal differences between Breton were less important in causing the break than Breton's normative insistence upon these differences and his demand for loyalty and obedience. Both positions involved a paradoxical relation between the objective and the banal on the one hand and the subjective and fantastic on the other. And besides, there was a shared concern to shatter the appearances of reality by what was either hidden from view (a reality to be revealed) or unconscious (a reality to be uncovered).

Painlevé and Franju were primarily documentarists, recording what existed and finding within it the strange and the dreamlike, seahorses in the one case, the abattoirs of Paris in the other. Most of Painlevé's films have a 'scientific' and pedagogical sense: the life cycle of sea urchins, crabs, seahorses and a celebration of the wonders and visual abstractions of these processes, thus connecting Painlevé's films to the European avant-garde of the 1920s and 1930s and its concerns with visual and graphic form: colour, movement, rhythm, syncopation, line, temporality, the interaction and overlapping of different realities and materials as in collage. His films followed a path already delineated in the works of René Clair, Jean Cocteau, Viking Eggeling, Jean Epstein, Abel Gance, Hans Richter and Dziga Vertov.

Painlevé's commentary for *Le Sang des bêtes* is probably chiefly responsible for the juxtaposition in the film of different elements: blood and water, dance and slaughter, steam and clouds and, above all, the disturbing, because grotesque and parodic, singing of Charles Trenet's immensely popular 1946 song *La Mer* as animal blood is collected into channels to flow from the abattoirs into the sewers of Paris. It is a poetics of opposites and juxtapositions that highlight each term and substance yet see them as a continuum, by which the one becomes the other and both made strange even shocking.

Painlevé's approach to film brought him closest perhaps to Vertov. What Painlevé 'sees' or more exactly what his camera 'sees', by its speeding up or slowing down of time, manipulating light and bringing about unlikely antithetic juxtapositions while objectively present are only visible by means of the camera, not the human eye. It is like Vertov's camera-eye that documents and is true yet goes beyond surface realities, an approach to image-documents reconfigured by montage between and within shots whose fundamental is the frame and whose essential gesture is deframing. It brings Painlevé close to the future French Nouvelle Vague and its insistence on style and the cinematic, what cinema alone can create (*mise en scène*), central for discovering, naming and idealising *auteurs*.

Elements in the Vertov film and their montage correspond to Surrealist chance encounters, like the deadly encounter in Jean Rouch's *Gare du Nord*, an episode in *Paris vu par* (1965), a film of episodes of encounters and encounters between episodes. For Painlevé and for Vertov ordinary reality was only apparent. It takes the eye of the camera to reveal true reality, what is behind or within 'mere' appearance. Painlevé, however, was concerned with revelation in nature, Vertov, with reconstruction and the machine.

The films are structured around encounters, some ruled by chance and coincidence, like unexpected, unlikely arrivals from out of another time and space, for example, in the films of Jean Renoir, the aviators in *La Grande illusion* (1937) and *La Règle du jeu* (1939) who appear almost by accident or as unexpected guests as in *Le Crime de Monsieur Lange* (1935), *The River* (1950), *La Carosse d'or* (1952), *French Can-Can* (1954), *Eléna et les hommes* (1956), involving misunderstandings, misrecognitions that shape and motivate the narrative, set them off, as if chance creates the plot rather than the plot having been plotted, the figures in a glass house or in a field whose embrace is spied upon by an eye-glass and misconstrued, leading to disaster as in *La Règle du jeu* and similar occurrences in *La Bête humaine* (1938).

The arrival of the new or unexpected into the familiar space of others is a difference that upsets the established, the social and the ritualised, or scandalises conventions, disrupts relations, uncovers secrets, ignores discretion and decorum – in short, violates order and the rules, makes the familiar unfamiliar, comical, farcical sometimes deadly, creating discomfort, danger and, by so doing, revealing 'other' hidden realities compounded of violence, jealousy, sadness, pride beneath the surface of unspoken assumptions and the good manners that sustain appearances and the illusions of life, the play of theatre and artifice, a reason that many Renoir films move along the edge of chaos.

Renoir, a contemporary of Painlevé, had – as Painlevé had – ties with the French avant-garde of the 1920s and 1930s, an avant-garde in which Surrealism was pre-eminent. The films of the French Nouvelle Vague, and especially perhaps, the films of Jean Rouch, have similar connections. Rouch and the Nouvelle Vague directors are all Renoirians and ... Hitchcockians. Jean-Luc Godard's *Nouvelle Vague* (1990) is a remake and citation, a homage to Jean Vigo's *L'Atalante* (1934), Hitchcock's *Vertigo* (1958), Chaplin's *The Great Dictator* (1940) and Renoir's *La Règle du jeu*, films of mistaken identities, of mirrors, of doubling, of sudden revelations, of interruptions and encounters where everything that was is effaced, negated becomes something else, of which Chaplin's film is particularly rich, Hynkel (Charlie as buffoon) nullified by the Jewish Barber (Charlie as poet).

Jean Painlevé had a privileged upbringing. His father, Paul Painlevé, was well known: a brilliant mathematician who did original work on differential equations and a powerful politician who held the cabinet posts of War and Finance in the French Government in the 1920s and 1930s. Jean Painlevé directly and indirectly was affected by the destructiveness of the First World War, the world depression at the end of the 1920s, avant-garde experiments of the interwar period, the rise of fascism, the political polarisation fascism entailed, the occupation of France by the Germans in the Second World War, the puppet Vichy government in the south of France, French collaboration with the German occupation and French complicity with Nazi policy toward the Jews, and a French Resistance movement that was relatively modest. Politically, Jean Painlevé was close to the avant-garde, to the French Left and to the Surrealists who, in varying degrees, were anti-fascist, either directly involved with or sympathetic to the French Communist Party (PCF). Such political loyalty by artists and writers raised a number of issues and questions for them and for Painlevé, namely what kind of art should one produce, what kind of culture strive for, in short, what were the social responsibilities of artists in the circumstances of fascism, competing ideologies, violence, misery, massacre and suffering – questions, interestingly enough, central to almost all of Godard's work from the 1990s to today.

The films Painlevé made (for the most part), he thought of as scientific and instructive. Their beauty and fascination was in nature, that is, in the real. Such a concentration on the real went beyond morality, interpretation, tradition, convention or psychology. It was reality seemingly stripped bare. If there is an ethic in his work, it is to be accurate – that is, to be true. The revelation of beauty was an extra, literally a super abundance, a sur-reality, the poetry inherent in the real and the desires it might provoke. It was unaccustomed combinations and juxtapositions that Painlevé's films displayed (as his commentary in the Franju film attests) where the dances and the giving birth by seahorses or sea urchins anthropomorphised them, thereby brought them close, made the tiny creatures living in mud seem almost human. It was not simply identification, but imagination and especially dream facilitated by the strange colours of the undersea, the transparencies and movements of the sea animals, dancing in another and mysterious world to the music of Jaubert, not unlike the character of Jean in Vigo's *L'Atalante* searching underwater for his lover in the river, then finding her miraculously as if in a dream of Atlantis. *L'Atalante* itself seems to have been dreamt and to be composed of dreamers dreaming.

Painlevé avoided the obscurity of the Surrealists (his figures were shrimps and octopus doing what shrimps and octopus normally do) or the abstractions and difficulties presented by the avant-garde in its reorganisations of space, its collages, condensations of time, evident distortion and disconnection as in Cubism and Dada. Painlevé's films were charming, fascinating, accessible and popular. They were distributed by the large movie companies and exhibited commercially. The films had elements of avant-garde formality and Surrealist ideas, but were not scandalous, obscure nor distressing. They skirted a line between innovation and the traditional, found distortions and the wonder of the real within reality and by associations (anthropomorphism). Rather than deforming (and often offending as with Buñuel), Painlevé simply (more or less) recorded and could claim and did claim truth and objectivity, also beauty and subjectivity: spectacle, fictionality, dream, harmonies, rhythms, the music of objects as issuing from reality and an identification and continuum between small creatures of the sea and the human such that their lives and gestures were mirrors of our own, as if sea animals were if not our doubles, our comrades.

The social and political situation in Europe (and America) in the 1920s and 1930s in part related to the Depression, in part to the appearance of right-wing movements (Nazism, Fascism and their accompaniments of racism, nationalism and anti-semitism), and in part to a militant Left (socialism and communism), whose tensions and differences were ignited in the Spanish Civil War and had positive consequences for the development of the documentary film and along two lines. One, it defined, indeed demanded, that the documentary be politically and socially committed (reveal injustice, condemn fascism, support the socially deprived and exploited), documentary that could be liberal, or politically radical and extreme. And two, because documentary in the broadest sense was outside the commercial industry and could be made for relatively little money (documentary films were usually short, had no stars and their technology and production were comparatively inexpensive and accessible), provided an opportunity for experiment, not simply in content (non-fictional, socially committed) and in forms and techniques. This situation brought together a social and political left and the artistic avant-garde. (This was also the case in America in which Orson Welles has an outstanding place.) Surrealism (and Dada) were symptoms of that conjunction and a response to it as were the films of Jean Vigo (À propos de Nice), Franju and Painlevé.

A corollary could be drawn in Painlevé's films between the marginalised fauna, crabs, shrimps and urchins in his films that he poeticised and the social realities of the period as if by seeing beauty in the neglected and despised (a view remarkably close to Pasolini's poetics and his sacralisation of the marginalised and socially scorned), was, as with Vigo, an indication of hope (in a future, of an ideal), and also an accusation against and condemnation of the present from the perspective of an idealised past combined with a nostalgia for a lost world. Because the subjects of his films and the forms they took were distant from and other than traditional, commercial films, dominant films that by extension represented dominant social forms and social classes, Painlevé's films introduced an otherness and opposition. Documentary as a form and practice could be thought of, potentially at least, as politically disruptive and socially committed because it was least institutionalised by its subjects and modes of production, more devoted to the 'real' than ordinary films were, and thereby a challenge to conventional fictionalisations of reality. In short, his films undermined the illusions of most films and of the society that produced and celebrated these films, hence the insistence on surprise and shock (Buñuel, Vigo, Franju, Marcel Duchamp), or on abstraction and formalisation (Viking Eggeling, Man Ray, Jan Epstein, and again Duchamp), by still others on lyricism and poetry (Vigo, Gance) – in any case, a refusal of convention and the established and a commitment to experiment and possibility and in the name of what was claimed to be not illusion, but truth and the real.

Attention to beasts and animals in 1930s films and later in Hitchcock's *The Birds*, for example, and Bresson's *Au hasard Balthazar* (1966), helped to create a cinematic bestiary: Painlevé's undersea creatures and his vampire bats, the pussycats in Vigo's *L'Atalante*, the cows, dead donkeys and dogs in the Buñuel-Dali films, the scorpions that open *L'Âge d'or*, the horses, cattle, lambs and calves slaughtered in Franju's *Le Sang des bêtes* and the killer dogs in his *Les Yeux sans visages*. And there is too Buñuel's *Un Chien andalou* (*The Andalusian Dog*) with its ants and Welles's story of the scorpion and the frog in *The Lady from Shanghai* (1947) and, in that film, the scenes in the aquarium, or Chris Marker's stuffed museum animals in *La Jetée* (1962), and, in Marker's other films, obsessions with cats and owls, the dying giraffe in *Sans soleil* (1983), the mythical animal monster of Jean Cocteau's *La Belle et la bête* (1946), Jacques Demy's *Peau d'âne* (1970), Merian Cooper and Ernest Schoedsack's *King Kong* (1933), the monster fish in Fellini's *La dolce vita* (1960) and the magical horses and cows that appear in his *La strada* (1954), *I Clowns* (1970) and *Amarcord* (1973), and Spielberg's *Jaws* (1975) and Eastwood's *Every Which Way but Loose* (1978). Animals, mostly dogs and horses, figure in every Buster Keaton film and particularly in *Go West* (1925) where he falls in love not with a young woman, but with a cow. The bestiary not only approaches the human and serves symbolic and aesthetic ends – in Painlevé's case almost 'purely' so – but also social and political ones while making possible a poetic bestiary, a sense of the marvellous even when horrible (bats, the abattoir, killer dogs, sharks), of the human aspect of beasts and the bestiality of humans, the way we and they resemble the 'other'. The beasts and their performances are objectively real and concrete while they add a sense of an extra reality, the fantastic combined with our projected subjectivity, the real, the animal and our desires.

Painlevé's original commentary for *Le Sang des bêtes* had the animals 'speaking' in the first person, narrating their happy lives in the countryside just before being put to death as if witnesses of their own extermination (like the Jews in the camps). Franju tells the story of the smiling man undergoing brain surgery, how happy he seemed while remaining conscious as the surgery progressed and how fascinating, beautiful and compelling the details of the medical procedure were of the inside of the brain. Franju was interested in the double contrast, closeness and reversibility between the beautiful and the horrible, the objective and the fascinating, life and death.

André Bazin tells a similar story and he adds to it another of the exquisite beauty of a cancerous lung during surgery where art, science, fiction and fantasy come together. His essay, written just after the war in 1947, *Beauté du hasard: Le film scientifique* is in praise of Jean Painlevé, in particular his film of the vampire bat, its combination of beauty and reality, grace, elegance and violence, Duke Ellington's music and the beasts, cuddliness and bloodsucking, a surreality of juxtapositions, as if each term served both to negate and establish the other.

What you realise as important and compelling in these films is the way they overcome and disrupt boundaries, definitions and fixities. It is in that operation, that politics and the aesthetic come together, the case, for example, in Godard's *Histoire(s) du cinéma* where the stability of objects, figures, images, sounds, identities, realities are put at risk, after which nothing much is secure.

Jean Vigo

Atlantis is a mythical place, first mentioned in Plato's dialogues in the fourth century BC. It is a kingdom, and like most imaginary kingdoms, perfect and lost. Plato (and others) insisted on the existence of Atlantis, but where and when remained vague, something longed for but unattainable, like a dream. Jean Vigo's *L'Atalante* (1934) is that kingdom at once present and if not lost, ineffable.

Jean and his crew – Père Jules and the cabin boy – and his new bride Juliette, take a journey on his river barge, the *Atalante*, but without, it seems, a clear destination. For Juliette, the *Atalante* becomes not a dream made true, but an everyday of boredom, loneliness, dullness and chores. When the barge reaches Paris, Juliette runs away, ordinary reality not only provoking dreams, but a flight from it.

The barge *Atalante* is immensely concrete, solid, palpable, like the river, the weather, fog and light, but also like these, intangible, as evanescent as its passengers, vivid in their reality and insubstantial like ghosts or the figures of dreams. The film shimmers between these dimensions as if every present has emerged from a past, every past from a present, reality as a dream and dreams intensely real. Going nowhere, being nowhere and the sense of an irreducible presence are qualities not simply of the story and its characters, but of the structure and sensation of the film, the everyday transformed, the ordinary and banal made extraordinary and lyrical: doing the laundry, shaving, dressing, speaking, rising in the morning, kittens, the cats listening to the gramophone, the joy of morning, the cold of water, the blank stare of misery. It is impossible once again not to think of Chaplin where objects are given not only new functions but poetic and fantastic ones, bread rolls become dancers, the factory assembly-line the stage for a ballet, a chocolate cake into a hat or Hitler into the clown Hynkel, and the clown Hynkel into the sublime Jewish barber.

Vigo's film is indifferent to continuity with all it implies of direction in space (the film goes nowhere), of a play of looks determined by points of view sutured together (there are few reverse shots), of a hierarchy of shots leading toward a dramatic unity (the film consists of discontinuous scenes) of an illusion of reality as fluid and singular (every object and scene veers off into the imaginary).

Vigo at once insists upon the concreteness of things and at the same time their lack of substance, as if everything, no matter how true and real, is unstable, as if while everything you see must be believed, nothing is material, rather an image, a vision, a dream and a projection. Juliette finds Jean in a reflection in water and we find both as images in a film, equally reflections. He is her dream and they are our dream. Juliette lived in a narrow provincial (and absurd and grotesque) village in rural France. The *Atalante* and Jean were dreamlike to Juliette, a world in movement, open, glittering, exciting, marvellous and unknown, an Atlantis on water. What confronts her instead is the tedium and habits of work, the unease of the crew, the quotidian and its chores, Jean's abrupt changes of mood, his jealousies, temper, seriousness and sense of duty. Père Jules, the most preposterous, clownish and anarchic character, successfully transforms the restricted space of his overcrowded cabin into a magical world, the world Juliette had desired, but this time, it is in a cabin of disjoined objects each filled with memories and stories, years of travel and adventure to seemingly everywhere, above all to freedom and imagination. It is for that reason that Jean in a fit of jealousy and frustration, finding

Juliette in the cabin, smashes the objects of Père Jules and the dreams they contain.

If the cabin of Père Jules is limited by its frame and each object in it framed, the imaginary it evokes is not exactly to an out-of-frame and off-screen, but to dreamlike everywhere. Imagination is an escape by transforming what is framed and that only the camera and the cinema can accomplish.

When Juliette runs off and appears to be hopelessly lost to Jean, as if unrecoverable, the two forever separated, she by her desires, he by his loneliness and jealousies. Jean re-finds Juliette, but only as an image, by diving into the river from the barge, seeing her reflection from their immediate past (she is dressed as a bride) projected back into the present by way of a future. When Père Jules finds her at last, Juliette is listening to music, the music associated with her love affair with Jean when daily life had been music and poetry, and at that moment in the seedy café Père Jules, hearing the music that had marked Jean and Juliette as inseparable at the beginning of the film, finds her. He hauls her back to the *Atalante* and to Jean.

Music in the film is everywhere (the dance, at the café, on the radio, by the accordion, the phonograph, the singing) and it is with music that the film takes off and takes flight, as in the magical scene when Père Jules seems to make a record play with his finger, only to find, more magically still, that it is the accordion being played by the cabin boy, momentarily off-screen. This sense of an 'off', an elsewhere, another world of magic is in every shot, every image of the 'real'.

The music is elusive, interruptive, fugitive, taking hold of reality, but only for an instant, like a note or motif and then transports the film, characters and itself into another realm entirely, in effect into music.

In most films, every shot is programmed into an arranged structure where editing is an operation of integrating shots into a previously determined edifice such that there is nothing more to find, nothing not known beforehand to encounter, only something to illustrate. What occurs in *L'Atalante* is based on separate, individual, stunning shots, beautiful and marvellous in themselves and self-sufficient with a beginning and end and made of an interior tension and wavering between concrete reality and the lyrical and dreamlike, whose overall place in the film will come later, as in Juliette's incredible return to Jean and their joyous embrace full of desire. It is as if the film is found (rescued, restored) at the last moment, and like the voyage of *the Atalante*, its characters, wandering wide-awake in their dreams.

There is a resonance in Godard's *Nouvelle Vague* (1990), not only with Hitchcock's *Vertigo* (1958) but with *L'Atalante*. The three films are like fairy tales, the prince or princess seemingly by resemblance emerging (resurrected) from the deep. These are films that concern finding images (poetry, lyricism, fantasy, the imaginary) and of treasuring the discoveries having come upon them by chance rather than design, by projected wish and desire, in part by the transformation of reality not exactly into images but by means of images, the dead coming back to life, Madeleine/Judy snatched from the waters of San Francisco Bay, Juliette seen by Jean under the water returning to the *Atalante*, Roger Lennox, apparently drowned coming back as Richard Lennox and the mythical lost Atlantis, a barge on the river Seine

Jean Vigo died at the age of 29 from tuberculosis. He made only four films: two documentaries, *À propos de Nice* (1930) and *La Natation de Jean Taris* (1931) and one short feature, *Zéro de conduite* (1933) and a full feature, *L'Atalante*. Each film is a masterpiece and *L'Atalante* is one of the most beautiful films ever made.

The ostensible subject of *La Natation de Jean Taris*, a film only a few minutes long, is a study of the swimming technique of Jean Taris, a world Olympic record-holder and an unrivalled record-holder in France with nearly 29 medals earned in various swimming events. An ordinary person, Taris, goes into a swimming pool and is transformed into pure motion. The water, as he moves through it, becomes a play of bubbles and waves of light, like music or dance, and Taris, by the magic of the camera, worthy of Vertov and his image manipulations in the camera, emerges from the water fully dressed, lifts his hat to the camera (and audience), an ancient mythical god reincarnated as a bourgeois. As Taris is transformed into the abstraction of pure movement (while remaining Taris), the water is transformed into a play of light and waves (while only water) and the swimming pool into another and fabulous world, an underwater set for a ballet (while only a swimming pool), not unlike the momentary and exquisite transformation of the Seine into a river of memories and Jean and Juliette into pure reflections in *L'Atalante*.

Vigo breaks up the movement of Taris into its effects in the water as he divides up the parts of Taris's body (head, arms, legs, mouth, eyes) to create a new subject of fluidity and perpetual movement, a *natation* of images. The film wavers between boundaries, its ability not only to transform, but to exhibit the transformation that alters both Taris and temporality and space, exactly what occurs when Jean dives into the Seine in pursuit of a dream image of Juliette, to become like a dream image himself, suspended in water. When Taris doffs his hat, he is himself and someone else, an imaginary other, a reality and an image, overlapped, superimposed as occurs in the fade in/fade out at the end of the film. It is impossible not to think of Jean Painlevé's seahorses.

Nice is a resort town in the South of France on the French Riviera in Provence, a town for the *bourgeoisie* to holiday, relax, play tennis, promenade, ride horses, flirt, display themselves and most of all, to gamble. *À propos de Nice* was made during the annual Nice festival, a time of parades, mock life-size dummies, masquerades, parties, crowds – in other words, the grotesque, making-up, self-parody, the *bourgeoisie* at play resembling themselves as dummies on parade. Vigo, not unlike Franju, activates a series of contrasts, but not as with Franju, to see these differences coalesce and find in that coalescence the banality of horror, but to see each as a commentary on the other, the *bourgeoisie* and ordinary people, the rich and the poor, those served and those serving, a beautiful place filled with ugly people, their flesh and ageing bodies made disgusting, disintegrating, shadowed by disease and mortality. Nice, the playground, becomes Nice the cemetery, Nice, the city of liveliness, a mortuary of death and decay (of a class, of a society), though nothing is 'said'. Instead, the images, editing, montage and its juxtapositions speak to make the real unreal, the natural unnatural, the decent pornographic.

The film presents Nice as nastier than it proposes itself to be, like the lady dressed in lovely gowns, then seen naked, her flesh no longer firm, her breasts sagging, not seductive nor desirable, flesh on display as in a butcher shop. She is 'stripped' by the camera and by the editing in a consecutive yet make-believe time or is made to resemble the monstrous puppets in the festival parade, as if these and the *bourgeoisie* on the Promenade des Anglais are mirror images and indistinguishable.

The film is a dance of death.

Georges Franju

Georges Franju was a scenic designer for the theatre. In his mid-twenties, in 1935, he founded with Henri Langlois the Cinémathèque Française in Paris which grew out of the Paris film club movement where copies of films were collected and screened. In 1938, Franju became the Executive Secretary of the Fédération Internationale des Archives du Film (FIAF). Like Langlois, Franju was a *cinéphile*. His love for the cinema involved not only preserving film and exhibiting it, but thinking about it historically, that is, film not primarily for what it might represent or its subject, but rather in its relation to other films and thereby in relation to forms. Every film found, preserved and exhibited not only brought the past to the present, but reconfigured the entire history of film as if that history were starting all over again.

Unlike Langlois and more like the generation that succeeded theirs (the Nouvelle Vague critics and film-makers of the 1950s), Franju first became a film-maker of short 'documentary' films (ten in all) between 1935 and 1958, of which the best known are *Le Sang des bêtes* (1949) and *Hôtel des Invalides* (1951). After 1958 until 1974, Franju made eight feature films, of which the best known are *Les Yeux sans Visages* (1959), *Thérèse Desqueyroux* (1962) and *Judex* (1963).

Franju's films relate to two traditions in French film culture. One is so-called poetic realism of the 1930s of which Marcel Carné and Jean Prévert best represented a poetry of the everyday in an atmosphere of regret, melancholy and loss, centred on an urban working class and *petit bourgeoisie* and notable for a concern with 'realistic' settings and shadowy moods (ports, canals, the street, night, fog, drizzle, small hotels), though it was a realism almost wholly constructed and staged, settings for melodramas of failed love and doomed lives that gave to its realism (pictures of a scorned class, of low life in poor settings) a 'poetic' effect.

The second is French Surrealism of the 1920s, particularly evident in French literature and painting, though the Surrealists later embraced film for its combination of the real (the photographed image) and the possibility of uncovering within its images an unconscious, dreamlike unreal in discontinuous, contrasting, unusual and often shocking combinations. French Surrealism valued not only the mysterious, dreamlike and fantastic, the 'other' side to reality (surreality), but an everyday manifested not in high culture (which it rejected) but in 'low' culture – that is, from a *bourgeois* perspective, a despised, popular culture of the lower classes, scandalous, despicable, worthless, criminal, even perverse and forbidden because it violated norms of correctness, rationality, decency and conformity. Like poetic realism, French Surrealism found beauty in the rejected, the neglected and the mean. The link, much later, with the poetry, novels and films of Pier Paolo Pasolini is unmistakable.

Franju's films relate to both these traditions. He established, if not something entirely new to the French cinema, seemingly so, a cinema of the fantastic and of horror presented by Franju coldly, blankly, as if nothing out of the ordinary, the strange as natural, normal, acceptable and thereby all the more disturbing. Franju's work, like that of Alain Resnais, is also heir to a silent-film tradition that includes the serial films of Feuillade and the comedies of Chaplin and Keaton.

Le Sang des Bêtes takes place in the two main *abattoirs* at the fringes of Paris (at Villette and Vaugirard), at its gates (Porte de Pantin, Porte de Vanves) and at intersections of bridges, canals (canal de Ourcq), railways that transport the animals (horses, cattle, calves, lambs) to slaughter as well as the area surrounding the *abattoirs* (the markets and streets of Villette and Vanves) where children play, people live, lovers embrace oblivious to the death at their doorstep, like the life of German villages and towns bordering the death camps.

There are two settings to the film. One is at the outside of the *abattoirs*, the normal life of the city, which is light, lyrical, ordinary, banal and open and the inside of the *abattoirs* which are dark and theatrical, closed like a set and like it seeming artificial. The theatre is a theatre of death.

In the theatre of death, animals are killed, cut open, gutted, skinned, washed, decapitated, aerated, their heads and hooves stacked and stamped, their innards and carcasses hung, dripping, secured to hooks onto which they are hoisted. There are three elements to the slaughtering in the film: the flow of liquids (blood, water, the drains, the hosing down), the steam (the breath of the animal victims and of those who slaughter them, the steam from the hot blood that rises up in the slaughter rooms), the cutting up of the animals including decapitation (the fragmentation of bodies). The entire animal is sliced up into pieces and these in turn become at once 'fluid' and autonomous, not only 'freed' from the body, but free to associate elsewhere having been transformed into liquid, steam, clouds, glue, much like images might be liberated from purposes of representation, to become both abstract and material.

The 'documentation' of death moves in two directions, apparently opposed (and juxtaposed), but in fact part of each other: the ordinariness and 'reality' of the slaughter. The men simply fulfil a task and Franju simply 'reports' it, coldly, with neutrality and objectivity, only facts, like the 'facts' in the death camps in Resnais's *Nuit et Brouillard* (1956). On the other hand, there is the 'unreality' of what is taking place, unreal not because it is marked as such, but to the contrary, 'unreal' because matter-of-fact, death and slaughter and cruelty not exceptional but normal, the act of cutting off the head of a calf as casual as lighting a cigarette or, as on the 'outside' of the abattoir, as playing ball, kissing a girl, going shopping, the dawn of the day, the smoke of a train puffing by. It is not the contrast or not exactly the contrast of inside and out, theatre and reality that is marked but their indifference, their fluidity and instability in relation to each other, so that each, because contrasted, are all the more noticeable, the film creating a continuity and disrupting it almost simultaneously and by the same means, by a *montage*, the manner for example in which the steam of the slaughter rooms are, by association, absorbed by or constitute the smoke from the steam engine of a train, the clouds in the sky, and the fog; the blood and canals of blood and water flow into the Canal Ourcq. The involuntary twitching of slaughtered animals are like the gestures of ordinary life (an orgasm), or a kind of dance, a grotesque yet beautiful choreography, as in a burlesque or musical chorus line, the twitching of the hooves of the lambs perfectly coordinated and rhythmic. It is precisely the fragmentation, stressed by such juxtapositions and by the fact of cutting, excising, irrigating, decapitating that enable elements both to join and associate, to separate and disperse as happens in the structure of the film with its conjunctions of fragments of the 'realistic' and the 'theatrical', a montage of death. The horror comes primarily by the beauty, lyricism and interest of what is presented, an aesthetic purity and poetry brought to abstraction composed of blood and hooves, the twitchings of death, the sounds of terror and disturbances, all in a day's work.

Jacques Tati

Jacques Tati made only six films: *Jour de fête* (1949), *Les Vacances de Monsieur Hulot* (1953), *Mon Oncle* (1958), *Playtime* (1967), *Trafic* (1971), *Parade* (1974). In *Les Vacances de Monsieur Hulot, Mon Oncle, Playtime* and *Trafic*, Tati played the character Monsieur Hulot. The character has a blank expression, a shuffle walk, great delicacy, wears a raincoat, has trousers that are too short and that show his socks, a pipe always in his mouth and a hat on his head. Hulot is exceedingly normal, so much so as to seem unreal. Tati's first three films were exceptionally well received and popular. *Playtime*, however, which took him nine years to make, was a critical success only. It financially ruined him.

Whereas all his films depend on the quality of finding the comic in the ordinary, the absurd in the everyday, *Playtime* moves in a slightly different direction, toward the abstraction latent in concrete things, of ideas in matter, the general in the particular, forms in the ordinary, part of an oscillation characteristic of the French cinema between the popular (entertainment) and the modern (obscure, difficult, intellectual). In the earlier films of Tati, the anomaly between the real and unreal was not less marked, but rather less abstract than in *Playtime* and therefore perhaps more accessible.

Hulot is an observer of everyday life. There is no *weight* to his observations as if everything is interesting but nothing significant: the sound of waves at the seaside, the shouts of children, the arrangement of chairs, the emptiness of the beach, balloons in the air, lunchtime at the hotel, singing, the sound of the gramophone, the sight of a dog, a wagging tail, a piece of paper, the grass, the impatience of waiters, the behaviour and look of others, a moustache, a gait, the arrangement of clothing or of hair.

The combination of insignificance and importance is realised by various means. No event or occurrence is taken to a conclusion, no character is developed, occurrences are cut short, understated, subject to a constant reticence and delicacy in order not to go too far. Between one thing and another there is no apparent development, conclusion or continuity, nor is it possible to designate with clarity the nature of a scene since dramatic borders, direction or intent are lacking. Tati establishes a fluidity of one thing toward another while at the same time insisting on their lack of connection. There is hardly a story, not even the smallest (the gag) goes to a designated end. Even laughter is subdued. The films are extreme only in their discretion, a lack of emphasis, of saying more by saying less, of indicating the presence of things by their absence, sounds with no visible source, a view dependent on a sound but one that cannot be precisely placed or that seems irrelevant. Tati's humour depends upon the constancy of anomalies, everything at once believable and strange, appropriate and absurd. His immediate heir and who worked with Tati (and Bresson, Jerry Lewis and Oshima) is the clown Pierre Étaix, whose films, made in the 1960s, have only just (2010) been released in France.

Hulot never reacts. He, along with everything and everyone are filmed at a distance: no close-ups (not ever), no dramatisation (not ever), no stress or highlighting (not ever) and as a result a seeming non-involvement, non-acting. Hulot's principal role is as a disinterested observer of himself and of situations. Even when views might be thought of as subjective, they have no psychological resonance, no character to which they attach. Either Hulot is seen from the back or his face is covered or obscured. There is no guidance to an audience, nor interpretation, nor apparent manipulation, instead an obsessive concern for details which makes everything exceedingly realistic, concrete and believable, but lacks significance or clear location, therefore events seem unreal because unrelated and discontinuous. Every gesture is not only autonomous, but so radically as to be disconnected, only a fragment. It is these non-relations and the gaps they presume and create that make his films amusing.

Comedy depends on the subversion of the normal order of things. The world is going on in its usual course until it is in some way disrupted. In that disruption, the disturbance of the normal, a tear in its fabric, the fiction takes shape. The fiction is the story of the disruption and its consequences.

Terror in Hitchcock's films is intimately connected to this unravelling of the ordinary in comedy, the world gone awry and therefore frightening. Comedy is often violent and anarchic, particularly the comedy of clowns, breaking apart the acceptable and the normal often by caricature and exaggeration, slapstick, smashing, exaggeration, and taking pleasure in the result, the fall of someone or something where nothing is left standing, the perennial banana skin. Usually, the outcome is known in advance, like Hitchcockian suspense, and thus in essence its subject is more than it is, in excess of what eventually occurs. Tati is a master of timing, but his is an exactness of miscalculations (quite different from Chaplin), such that Hulot's efforts seeking to be just right are usually too little, too soon, too late, both too much and not enough, a kind of graceful inadequacy of excessive delicacy, discretion too far.

Tati does not introduce elements that overturn things. Hulot does nothing in particular except watching what others do and attempting with his extreme discreteness to be of use, to help out. But it is his grace and reluctance that causes trouble because it has its own rhythm to that of others and to that of the world such that every attempt to make things better, makes them worse, by a kind of overconcerned compensation and the world of order (to which Hulot, as if otherworldly, an alien from another planet, does not belong) begins to disintegrate because Hulot realises that everything considered to be socially important – rules, conventions, habits, relations – are not important, but are empty, insignificant, and if regarded intently the emptiness is revealed and the world simply falls apart. Hitchcock has that regard, but in his case, the issue and scene are less comic than guilty and often dirty, criminal and perverse. The terror of Hitchcock, however, is that these boundaries are porous. The pure is close to the dirty, the normal to the perverse, the comic to the shameful.

Such disintegration around a void is not simply contained in what is narrated, but is structural. Central to the composition of Tati's films is their lack of continuity, causation, development, hierarchy, sense, chronology, significance, of time itself (or at least the time of the chronometer), of tasks, responsibilities, 'purposes'. Even the dogs in his film have an indifference to risk and consequence. Hulot regards with great affection the nothingness of everything, the tempo of life and its surprises.

From *Playtime* onward, Tati's films become less funny (there is little to make one laugh in *Trafic*) and more beautiful. What they reveal as a displacement of the normal is something truly sublime, patternings of sounds, the appearance of geometric shapes, the serialisation of objects, a fluidity of time as if lack of purpose is the beginning of something fragile, tender and intensely beautiful, the movements, colours, tempo and resonances of things. It is an everyday differently regarded for its wonder and magic, its abstractness and its forms, in short, for its poetry and grace. Tati himself, like the best of comedians, is a Surrealist.

In *Les Vacances de Monsieur Hulot*, Hulot gives his attention to a young, very pretty woman, but nothing comes of it. The eroticism is so delicate, considerate, discrete, reserved and shy that it is never fully concluded as when Hulot, reluctant to touch the woman's back as they dance, places one finger instead, tentatively, on her halter neck collar. The sensibility of temptation and avoidance, desire and withdrawal, is also the source of gags involving his help with the woman's luggage, his waiting for her in the lounge where he disrupts the pictures on the wall and the objects at the piano and on the floor by attempting to put them just right, and the more absurd gag in the film with the horse and the car. This same erotic, sexual reticence is a quality of *Playtime* and central to its humour.

In Tati's films everything somehow seems suspended, arrested in time and understatement and, despite often frantic movements bordering on chaos, everything appears frozen or immobilised. He is fond of the *litote*, the less of things that say more, calling attention to something by not speaking of it or even representing it, *preterition*. His reserve is inordinate, hence he appears to be more English (whose better part is that of discretion) than he does French.

The real is treated by Tati in two manners with the same result. Either the particularity of things is stressed to utmost fidelity (the summer resort, the pictures on the wall, the elements, clothing, games, gestures, objects) that carry them beyond the real toward a seemingly too real, too precise, too normal to be believed (like Hulot himself), as if the development of the world has proceeded in one direction while Hulot has stood his ground. Everything in *Les Vacances* is so clear and precise and Hulot's attention so obsessive as to highlight insignificance, extreme yet inappropriate gestures of getting things that amount to nothing just right, as with the pictures on the wall or the search for the ping pong ball or the imitation of the tennis service on the court in imitation of what Hulot had learned at the sports shop. The other approach is a simplification, a stripping away of things to their formal essence – the arrangement of bathers in the water, of the cabins on the deserted beach, of the tennis players as if posing – such objects, persons and scenes begin to assume abstract qualities of pattern, shape and duration. In both instances, the stress on fidelity or the obsession with the simple, the real seems to lose all substance by perpetual understatement and incompleteness. Hulot is a *metteur en scène* of the greatest exactitude and will to perfection, hence his incompetence. Tati, on the other hand, carefully follows his invention, delighting in the inappropriateness of perfection that he perfectly stages.

The way in which the unreal takes flight from the real by means of an excessive fidelity or formality and simplification is part of other similar contradictions at play in the films of Tati, that of restraint and care turning to chaos, the concern with logic and rightness becoming illogical (the horse incident, the card-playing gag), the irrationality of the rational (the scheduling of events at the hotel, especially dining times) and the absurdity of the significant and the everyday (taking photographs, mistaking views, the gag with paint bucket, the creaking of the dining-room door, the sudden sound of music). Fundamentally, and with great attention, all things turn into their opposite. The result is almost always the destruction of order, a fluidity of time in a scheduled, mechanised universe of tasks and labour, a genius for the inopportune, the untimely and the discrete that invades a world constructed on other principles, to the point of a filmic and compositional reserve of irresolution, things left hanging, feet in the air, events and stories halted, situations interrupted, nothing finalised. Tati's genius is to make films of useless gestures, a genius for the inappropriate, where precision is the engine of catastrophe.

Raymond Depardon

Profils paysans (*Farmer Profiles*) is a film divided into three chapters made by Raymond Depardon and Claudine Nougaret centred on the lives of small farmers in the Cévennes region in south-eastern France along the Massif central. The area is mountainous and hilly, the farms isolated, set on the steep slopes of the Massif. The only farming possible on such land is husbandry, the raising of cattle, sheep and goats, but herd size is limited by the terrain. Holdings are small and the land unproductive for large-scale commercial agriculture or breeding. In short, farming is marginal and no longer profitable, left behind by current agriculture, yet labour-intensive.

Existence is difficult in the Cévennes and the way of life of its farmers doomed to extinction, casualties of *La Vie moderne*. The few remaining farmers in the Cévennes are old and frail, herds are dwindling, the scrub is taking over the hillsides, the land is exhausted and the farmers more so. Villages have turned into hamlets and hamlets have disappeared. The area is depopulated, while young people, sons and daughters, cousins, nieces, nephews of older farmers, have little incentive to carry on working the land. A critical problem for the farmers of the Cévennes is their legacy: to whom will they pass on the land, who will inherit their earth and their labour? The land is giving out and the people giving up. Many farmers are in their eighties either still working or unable to work and slowly they are dying off.

The subject of *Profils paysans*, as with nearly all of Depardon's films, is the neglected, the peripheral, the forgotten, those lost at the borders of modern life, victims of new institutions, of the law and of changes inherent in life itself. *Profils paysans* is a film concerned essentially with time.

Claudine

Claudine Nougaret has been the producer and sound engineer on most of the films usually credited exclusively to Depardon (almost 40 films). In fact, her role has been central and not only for the recording of sound and the details of production, but for overall planning, execution, solution of problems, mapping of strategies, making contact, organising and finance. Nougaret's contributions are especially valuable because Depardon-Nougaret films are settings for the spoken word, for sound and dialogue, the area where she is most skilled. The films take place in court rooms, offices, police stations, kitchens, dining rooms, corridors, waiting rooms, hospitals, insane asylums, prisons, where they are set, put in scene. One way or another, literally or figuratively, those filmed are constrained, handcuffed, made inmates or patients because of the rooms in which they are placed and because of the situations in which they find themselves; in either case, they are unable to move, to extricate themselves. Much of the success and structure of the films are dependent on Nougaret's abilities as a sound engineer working in a confined space in direct sound and necessarily attentive to the duration of shots in relation to the duration and sense of speech (editing and cutting are minimal) and the way in which image and sound seek out the slightest gestures and intonations of the persons filmed.

Depardon and Nougaret are married, a film-making couple, like Jean-Marie Straub and Danièle Huillet, Johan van der Keuken and Nosh van der Lely and, since the early 1970s, Jean-Luc Godard and Anne-Marie Miéville. Depardon is the son of small farmers near Villefranche-sur-Saône, north of Lyon and to the north of the Cévennes. His childhood and happiest memories are connected to the farm (*La Ferme du Garet*). The couple, Depardon-Nougaret, is not dissimilar from a farming couple toiling together with limited means and strong passions, sensitive to accident, skilled at improvisation, dealing with obstacles, like Depardon's parents and the farmers he speaks with in *Profils paysans*. There is something old-fashioned and reminiscent of the couple.

In an interview with Depardon and Nougaret in *Cahiers du cinéma*, Nougaret indicated that the project for *Profils paysans* was fifteen years in the making.[1] The three chapters are *L'Approche* (2000), *Le Quotidien* (2004) and *La Vie moderne* (2008). Between the film(s) and their life there is not much difference.

Photography

Depardon became interested in photography on the farm while in his early teens. His photos were of the farm, its courtyard, the stone steps leading to the grange, his parents, relatives, friends, dogs, livestock, the hidden places of the farm that were 'his', the attic in the barn, where he developed his photographs. At 14, he was apprenticed to an optician-photographer in Villefranche. Two years later he left the region (the farm, his parents, his childhood, the optician) for Paris where he found work at the photographic agency Magnum as a *pigiste*, a piece worker, paid per photograph used. Soon Depardon was employed on staff full-time at Magnum, salaried as a reporter-photographer. He followed the news, current events, persons (celebrities, politicians) that were deemed significant (newsworthy, notable) by the agency which sold its photographs to journals, magazines and newspapers, acquiring in the process an immense archive of sold and unsold images to be marketed later when conditions were favourable. Depardon in fact less followed the news than was led by it, determined by it, dictated to by it. Going through his own photographs in the archives,

Depardon noticed that for him the most interesting ones were least significant for the agency or its clients. What was thought significant (hence commercial) had little meaning for Depardon and seemed – as current notoriety often is – ephemeral, both important and trivial at once.

Depardon not only felt distant from the significant, but he had little appetite for the poetic (a beautiful landscape), the romantic (the peasantry) or the meaningful (a humanism), for these kinds of rationales and ends. Robert Frank, the American photographer, was most admired by Depardon, especially Frank's photographs taken of New York, for their honesty and directness, even brutality, quite different from the 'model' for French photography (and beyond France) of the work of Henri Cartier-Bresson: '... l'Amérique de Cartier-Bresson est plus traditionnelle, plus romantique, au fond un peu fausse' ('...the America of Cartier-Bresson is too conventional, too romantic, essentially a bit false').[2]

For Depardon, the photographs of photo-journalism were a constraint, an institutional demand, not something personal, not like the 'free' photographs young Depardon had taken on the family farm and for no apparent reason save his interests, fascination and what he loved. Such photographs – personal, insignificant, marginal – were more compelling for him and more open than the closed 'official' images imposed by photo-journalism and that defined it. This kind of conventional photography has been criticised and analysed in the writings of Roland Barthes for their dishonesty and by Jean-Luc Godard and Jean-Pierre Gorin in their *Letter to Jane* for their ideology, all the more pernicious for being hidden by an appearance of truth, reality and objectivity, in short by reportage, an entire industry of dishonest image-production. Depardon's attraction to what was peripheral, what might be thought to be 'empty', that is, without a 'subject', was outside the pertinent, habitual, nameable, expected, beautiful and definable. These margins became the 'subject' of his later photographs, at once personal (his presence could be felt), a veering from the 'objective' (without losing reality), no longer subservient to the agencies, a commitment both to the everyday and often the unnoticed or ignored. As photography went in the late 1950s and early 1960s, Depardon was not alone. He photographed the unspeakable, not integrated, the displaced: criminals, the insane, the sick and the old farmers of the Cévennes. The images Depardon produced as photographs, with words and on film were 'weak', nothing totalised, no imposed dominant voice or sight. Their weakness, an apparent lack of framing, and a disjunction between words and images, such that neither the one nor the other functioned to illustrate or explain, became also a strength of his films. His photographs were neither reportage nor militancy nor poetry but their negation.

> 'Je pense encore aujourd'hui, sincèrement que le photographe n'est pas un journaliste' ('I still sincerely believe that the photographer is not a journalist').[3]

The 'I'

The photographs of photo-journalism involve a tautology: what is noted is notable, what is not noted, not notable. The mayoral election campaign of Jacques Chirac, for example, was noted and so noted it became notable and because it was notable, it was noted. Reporters were sent out to take notice. Such photographs are essentially fictional based on the fiction that what is referred to 'in' the photograph is external to the picturing of it, the photographic images thereby objective, reproducing what is in front of it, as if not 'I', but reality, the referent, has determined the image, while the subject of the image, what is reproduced, effaces the image causing it and its author to disappear by its force and its conventionality (a figure, an event, the 'historical'). Instead of the 'I', still less a discourse, there is 'fact' and 'objectivity', perfect transparency achieved by a denial of presence as if nothing had been enunciated, nothing articulated, instead something recorded. In short, the photographs of photo-journalism present themselves (it is their pose) as undeniable testament: 'this has happened'. In doing so, negation, anything other than itself is denied and image and the reality so unified that reality seems to speak unaided, unformed, untouched.

It was this aspect of photo-journalism that Depardon found unacceptable, that isolated him, made him uneasy and unhappy, not only for the constraint of the subject, but for its apparent anonymity and falseness, its pretence at truth. Depardon's 'own' photographs, those in his books, books of photos and texts – around 30 titles to date – such as *Errance* (*Wandering*), *Le Tour du monde en 14 jours* (*Around the World in 14 Days*), *La Solitude heureuse du voyager* (*The Carefree Loneliness of the Traveller*), *Afrique(s)* (*Africa(s)*), *1968, New York, Paris Journal, La Ferme du Garet* (*Farm Garet*), *La Terre des paysans* (*Farmer's Earth*) are products of wandering without specific purpose or end, without a unity, unassigned, no goal except to wander, to depart, to be elsewhere and in the process to be open, aware, alert to the slightest murmurs of light and gesture to an unaccustomed path or association, a purposeless purpose that privileges encounters, chance, accident, the everyday, as if every journey were a journey to take oneself elsewhere, and, by going away, establish a distance in order to get close.

Such an enterprise is a valorisation of the *quotidien*, the indefinable, impalpable and unpredictable. It resumes the preoccupations of the modernist avant-garde of the 1920s and 1930s, of Surrealism, of Vertov, of Futurism, more to do with meetings of differences than assigned journeys of purpose and ends. Is Depardon not a *flâneur?*

Depardon's photographs are, like his films, non-informative, non-interpretative, and (in the films) mute. He asks questions, but refuses to be questioned. It is precisely his negations that keep his images autonomous, free, unlimited, associative and rebellious. It is something of a paradox that Depardon-Nougaret images are blank, frontal, fixed and of long duration, yet it is these qualities that make their work ambiguous, uncertain, diffident. What they affirm instead is the question, outsideness, what is 'other' and difficult to fix and categorise or accept: the lunatics in *San Clemente*, the distressed and confused in *Urgences*, the petty criminals of *Délits flagrants* and *Faits divers*, the farmers of the Cévennes in *Profils paysans*, an interplanetary road movie among aliens.

'here' and 'elsewhere'

Depardon's initial act of freedom at 14 years old was to leave the farm for the sake of photography if only to take himself a few kilometres away to Villefranche. It was the beginning of his journey, as it is with all of us, away from childhood. Depardon's sense of time however was not progressive. Childhood may have come first, his earliest and most pleasant experience, but it was never left behind, never passed by into 'maturity', consigned to the past and forgotten, not in Villefranche, not in Paris, never in all his wanderings and assignments as a photographer in North Africa, Black Africa, the African desert, the bush, other parts of Europe, the United States, New York, nor by his marriage to Claudine (the farmer couple!).

However far Depardon was from home, from the central courtyard at Garet, however elsewhere he was, and especially when he was elsewhere, he longed for home. At home, he longed to leave for elsewhere, to be a *voyageur* (traveller) and yet still remain a *casanier* (a stay-at-home), both identities at once, his body in one place, his thoughts and affections elsewhere.

One way to be a *voyageur* is to be an artist, to write, photograph, paint, compose, film, to lose oneself on the path to help find oneself yet always being elsewhere one way or another. ('I' is always 'other', for no other reason than that it is language and 'I' is less a reality than a structure of speech.) Depardon in his travels, either literally or by making things, was simultaneously close and distant, intimate and reserved, oneself and 'other', on the side of reality and on the side of the imaginary, both present in every image and word, nothing really lost, nothing cancelled, a paradox and a contradiction 'held', at the heart of *errance*.

The desert was an 'ideal' place for Depardon, perfect emptiness, and now and then an oasis, a *palmeraie*. He and Nougaret called their film production company *Palmeraie & Désert*. Returning from the African desert and arriving first in Marseilles, Depardon wrote: '... pour moi, aujourd'hui, le voyage est fini, il ne me reste plus qu'à remonter la vallée du Rhône, suivre les platanes et les tuiles romaines, arriver à Villefranche-sur-Saône, à la ferme Garet ... C'est ici que j'ai passé mon enfance, c'est dans cette cour que j'ai grandi, joué, photographié pour la première fois ('for me, now, the trip is over, all that remains is to go up the Rhône valley, follow the plane trees and the Roman roof tiles, arrive at Villefranche-sur-Saône, at the farm Garet ... It is here that I spent my childhood; it is in its courtyard that I grew up, played, took photographs for the first time).[4] The image of the courtyard is the last image of his book *Afrique(s)* and these comments its last words.

The sense of here and elsewhere is not strictly biographical or autobiographical, but the essence of Depardon's images, both photographic and cinematographic, where the real and the imaginary overlap. In that join and in the gap and difference between them, the two positions superimpose and touch one another, everywhere in *Profils paysans*, in every image, every word. Depardon takes his distance in fact in the Cévennes by fixed images, lengthy sequences, a regard literally from the outside, yet imaginatively being there, he is transported to home, to Garet, to its courtyard, to his childhood. It is the final image in his imagination and also the first, where he begins and where he returns, travelling down a road, accompanied by the music of Gabriel Fauré's mournful, melancholic *Élégie* (Opus 24), a refrain in the three chapters of *Profils paysans*. Like the Fauré music, the film is an elegy, as in Chris Marker's *Sans Soleil* (the title of a piece by Modest Mussorgsky and a homage to him) and *Le Tombeau d'Alexandre* (a homage to Maurice Ravel in the form of a *tombeau*).

At the end of the road in *Profils paysans* there is a farm of a farmer family (the Privat or Rougière or Brès or others) and also, imaginatively Garet and Depardon's childhood, his parents. The two locations superimpose, one present in reality, the other in memory, the one moving toward a future (of extinction), the other returning from the past (refreshed). In watching the 'other', the farmer families, so like Depardon's own and himself, as if traversing a mirror of time, passing to the other side like Orpheus does in Jean Cocteau's *Orphée* and the main character does in Marker's *La Jetée* is the experience of loss and of presence simultaneously, of being somewhere yet absent, of reality and its image, the end of a journey and its inception, the distance of death and its closeness, new yet familiar encounters and thus strange, uncanny (science) fictional.

By taking a path forward, by going toward places that recede in time and toward images of them that will survive, Depardon returns – and by the only means possible – from reality to the imaginary, from the distant to the close, from himself to 'I', then back again, nothing fixed. 'Mes parents étaient paysans. Ce monde rural m'habite toujours' ('My parents were farmers. The rural world is always alive in me').[5]

Mise en scène

> Les photos et le film, c'est vraiment deux choses différentes, d'ailleurs la photographie n'est pas une bonne école pour faire du cinéma, c'est même un peu antinomique (Photos and films are indeed two different things. Moreover, photography is not a good school for making films, on the contrary).

Following the twilight, autumnal, crepuscular ending of *La Vie moderne*, the final chapter of *Profils paysans*, the locations of the film are seen by a camera looking backward at the road that the film and Depardon-Nougaret have traversed for nearly fifteen years ('the most beautiful light of the most beautiful season of the year'). The film-makers take their leave of the Cévennes, accompanied by the Fauré *Élégie*. Each of the farmers that Depardon spoke with is presented in posed images as in a photograph, allowing us to go back in time (the time of their lives, of their own memories, the time of the film and its memories, the time of Depardon and his memories), to say goodbye to the characters, to the Cévennes and for the characters to bid us goodbye. The farmers in the three chapters and over a period of eight years (2000–2008), were the characters of *Profils paysans*, who played themselves, not quite Chaplin as 'Charlie', but certainly transformed into images and words, at once real (themselves) and fictional (played), a documentary but unavoidably a fiction. The two dimensions constantly encounter one another as the farmers encounter their images. They overlap, superimpose, neither effaced nor left behind nor left out.

Depardon and Nougaret carefully organised the shooting of the films. The settings have been selected as locations for 'words', laboratories for speaking: kitchens primarily, also dining-rooms, sometimes, less frequently, stables, and always the courtyards. The settings are where the theatre of the film 'takes place', where the film is literally 'played', 'performed' where the players assemble, where Depardon and Nougaret take their place and where the camera and sound-recording apparatus take theirs, positioned, unseen, out of frame, but heard and obviously present, and not only because Depardon engages the players in conversation, takes possession of the word, and Nougaret takes charge of recording to fit the sense of words, their duration and rhythms and to align them with the image, but also because the farmers/characters acknowledge the presence of the film-makers, the camera, the film and their own images, themselves and not themselves, here and elsewhere. Most often the characters sit at a table, facing the camera fixed in a central frontal position (there is no angularity) facing them. Sometimes, they address each other; more often, they address Depardon responding to his questions and in so doing address the camera whose view frames them from its fixed position, defining the borders of the shot and the distance between camera and subject. There is little if any 'point of view'. All shots are at once 'objective' by their fixity and 'subjective' by the clarity and presence of the *mise en scène*, the artifice of theatre (which always invokes a spectator), and, it might be added, the disturbance in the everyday of the farm and its family, of the real, provoked by Depardon and Nougaret's presence and the recording, the image-making in their kitchens choosing to whom to speak, who will listen, who will enter and who exit. To this extent, the film is stage-managed and Depardon an *auteur*. It is the film's fictional side.

On the other hand, the conversations, the gestures of the farmers have not been rehearsed, are not scripted, not dictated, nor their relations and words to each other. There is no attempt to illustrate words spoken or images pictured by these words nor are the words particularly dramatic or linked to the images (the absence of points of view, of sharp angles, of a varied frame, of counter-shots) – that is, the film does not offer, nor do the words, an 'interpretation', a weighting or hierarchy. In this regard, like Depardon, the film is mute despite all the words spoken. This 'side' of the film belongs to a tradition of *cinéma direct* much admired by Depardon (Robert Wiseman). It is essentially improvised within a preset *mise en scène*. Neither Depardon nor Nougaret is aware in advance of what will be said and to where what is said might lead. This is the 'documentary' side of the film, nevertheless encased in a road movie (fictional) where each pause at a farm introduces a new cast of characters or is a return to a former group, each pause a rhyme with the others including those in earlier chapters. By so doing the film and its stories (of characters and place and time) are extended or resumed.

The farmers as farmers are in the Cévennes and subject to it and as characters are in the images of these and images of themselves and in such a way as to resemble a Rivette film whose characters are caught and held by the intrigues and plots of their own invention or by circumstances out of their control, exactly the situation of the small farmers of the Cévennes narrating their own helplessness and inability to 'move', to get out of their reality and of its image.

The relations and interactions between the 'documentary'

Profils paysans and the 'fiction' *Profils paysans* are incessant and, though distinct, are so only temporarily. Their boundaries shift and are porous. One becomes the other and vice versa, thereby recalling the cinema of Rivette. Rivette encourages improvisation and then locks it into place in the script. Improvisation then *determines* the circumstances that come next. The improvised is a force and a limitation and can become of trap as if fiction lies in wait for the characters (and the actors who invent the characters). This Rivettian notion and practice echos the cinema of Howard Hawks whose films Rivette wrote about with great admiration, where characters are caught and confined in what seem to be impossible situations. The approach is close to, and perhaps more essentially, the cinema of Renoir.

I would like to speculate, though I have no evidence to support it, that Depardon-Nougaret are aware of such connections (they do live in Paris). Not only can one associate between them, Renoir to Depardon, for example, especially since Renoir – like Rivette – initiates a play between theatre and artifice on the one hand, and film, illusion and reality on the other, but these 'other' films function to interpret and 'read' other films still, like those of Depardon, however distant and unlikely they may seem, as Godard does in his films composed by resonances, citations, translations, transformations, transpositions (*Alphaville* is a permutation of John Ford's *The Searchers*, for example) while superimposed associations inform each other (and the audience).

Insofar as Depardon and Nougaret take part in their films, the recording of sound and the shooting of the film are 'real' presences, and like the farmers, they too are actors, who enter the fictional-documentary space of the film from a real-fictional space outside of it where they organise the *mise en scène*, but do so as a setting for improvisation and spontaneity (by themselves, by the camera, by the 'actors'), a staging of documentary until the staging itself as a performance (not what is staged) becomes paramount to the point where the long takes and fixed camera reveal their presence and gestures. They are devices to see and to hear within a space configured for encounters and reflections, for the conjunction not only of Depardon to Nougaret, but Depardon-Nougaret to the farmers of the Cévennes, of reality to fiction, actuality to memory, the farms at Lozère and the Ardèche to the farm of Garet (*un bout de cette cour*), to the childhood of Depardon, to his parents and to these farmers, all set at a just distance to be observed, and with a closeness to be shared. To be close and distant is a strategy and paradox central to Depardon. *Profils paysans* is an instrument to return home and to return to oneself and to bring cinema to the Cévennes.

Photography/film

It is tempting (and the temptation is usually not resisted) to see in the film-maker Depardon the shadow of the photographer Depardon. The evidence is in the testimonial, evidential, documentary aspects of his films, the long takes, the immobile camera, the frontality and the centrality of figures, a certain stillness, as if his films, among other things, belong to portraiture. Depardon, however, will have none of this.

Just as his photography is opposed to photo-journalism, so it is opposed to the cinema. The fact that both photography and cinema can be placed together because of their apparently similar views of duration and because both can be thought of as 'documentary', both 'record' what is set before it, what matters to Depardon is time. The long sequence shot is used not because it is on the side of photography, but because 'il vient de mes origines paysannes' ('it comes from my rural origins'),[6] best exemplified perhaps in the lyricism of *La Vie moderne*, of autumn twilight and the dead leaves of memory like the gathering up of moments of love, regret and melancholy, *Les feuilles mortes*, Marcel Carné, Jacques Prévert, Raymond Depardon and Gabriel Fauré. *Profils paysans* is a love song and an elegy.

Notes

1. Frodon 2008, pp. 10–17.
2. Depardon and Bergala 2006, p. 34.
3. *Ibid.*, p. 39.
4. Depardon 2010.
5. Depardon 2000, p. 86.
6. Frodon 2008, p. 17.

Alfred Hitchcock

Vertigo narrates a story of deceit, desire, hallucination and murder. Central to the story is the doubling of identities, the circularity of time, of similitudes, of mirror images and repetition. Identity in the film, in part, is a matter of the construction of character by clothes, specifically clothes as a lure, as fascinating, as making desirable (Madeleine for Scottie) and as a seeking to be adored (Judy as Madeleine).

In the film, dressing up (and undressing) occur principally in four scenes. The first, when Scottie (James Stewart) sees Gavin Elster's wife Madeleine (Kim Novak) at Ernie's, a fashionable restaurant in San Francisco, in a style in imitation of the past, an image of old San Francisco (the restaurant is also 'dressed up' to recall a past). The second, when Scottie, having rescued Madeleine after she jumped into San Francisco Bay, takes her, unconscious, to his home, undresses her, puts her to bed, hangs her wet clothing including stockings, lingerie and underwear in the kitchen to dry. The third, and the most terrifying, when Scottie, by chance, meets Judy (Kim Novak once again) on the street who resembles Madeleine with whom he had fallen in love, but is now dead. Madeleine had committed suicide by jumping from a church bell tower, a suicide for which Scottie feels responsible. He tries to turn resemblance (of his dead lover) into reality by making the vulgar Judy over again (new clothes, hairdo, accessories) to become (in his fantasy) the elegant and sophisticated Madeleine once more, a lost love. The fourth is when Judy (now looking like Madeleine) dresses up to go to dinner with Scottie to Ernie's (a return to the place where he first had met Madeleine and been fascinated by her and that begins his pursuit of her, or more precisely of an image of her).

Kim Novak, a Hollywood Star, that is, someone never herself in reality, who, even in real life always played a part, someone studio- and media-fabricated, is both Judy and Madeleine in the film (and also, obviously, Kim Novak, one of the many multiples of combined doubled identities in the film). Judy had always been Madeleine. She was constructed so by Gavin Elster to resemble his wife, to play the role of Madeleine (down to her underclothes) in order to attract, deceive and lure Scottie to make possible the murder of the true Madeleine by Elster with Scottie used as an alibi. In fact, Madeleine's death is a faked suicide by the false Madeleine played by Judy of the already murdered real Madeleine. Two deceits are involved: Judy posing as Madeleine, and murder posing as suicide. Scottie is deceived because he suffers from vertigo as a result of having witnessed the fall from a rooftop of a policeman who, with Scottie, was pursuing a criminal, and for whose death Scottie feels responsible, whose sign is his disability. Elster reckoned that Scottie would not pursue the false Madeleine up the steps of the bell tower as a result, and, because she and the true Madeleine resembled each other and wore the same clothes, Scottie (and the audience) would believe the false to be true, namely that it was Madeleine who jumped and died, a truth implied since there is no image of it until later in the film.

What Scottie and the audience see is true, but the truth is only apparent. Its real truth (the murder of Madeleine by Elster and the deceit of Judy to cover it) is masked by the projections, fantasy and intepretation of Scottie and the audience, both, by identification within the film – neither can go up the tower – and both also by identification, participants and observers, who interpret – mistakenly – what they see or don't see. Almost all of Hithcock's heroes are so doubled as actors and as observers (their own audience). Scottie is like Elster insofar as both of them dress Judy to make believe she is Madeleine, Elster as a conscious plot and design, Scottie as unconscious desire and unavoidable obsession. In the first instance, Scottie is fooled; in the second, it is he who makes Judy by dress, make-up and hairdo to be Madeleine, not only a love lost, but in fact a love never possessed, since Madeleine was never herself but only an imitation, an appearance.

The doubling is further complicated. Madeleine, as Elster relates to Scottie, is inhabited by Carlotta (the 'mad Carlotta'), Madeleine's great-grandmother who committed suicide in 'old San Francisco' when she was the same age as Madeleine now is and who, Elster said, would duplicate that suicide if left on her own unobserved, that is, Madeleine is doubly not herself: she is Carlotta and she is Judy, pursued by a fiction from the past and being pursued by Scottie as that fiction, at once horribly real in fact, and also only an image, fabricated, fictionalised, a fantasy being pursued and lived by Scottie. More exactly, Judy plays Madeleine who is made to seem someone possessed by Carlotta to the point where Madeleine-Judy not only visits the sites of old San Francisco, including the house where Carlotta lived, and stares at a portrait of Carlotta in a museum, but wears her hair like Carlotta in the portrait (in a spiral bun), buys a bouquet of flowers held by Carlotta in that portrait and wears the necklace as in the painting, the necklace Madeleine (the real Madeleine) had inherited from Carlotta – that is, Judy, who fakes being Madeleine, does so by having Madeleine live a fiction as Carlotta, and in great detail, particularly of clothing, accessories, hair style … to match an image with another image.

Carlotta, in turn, so the story goes as told to Scottie by the owner of an antiquarian bookshop, was herself 'constructed' by a rich man with power who had remade her from ordinary girl into a lady, had a child with her, then rejected her and kept the child. Carlotta was reduced to rags, went mad and killed herself. Elster (rich and powerful) remakes Judy, a shop girl of hideous taste and vulgar manner, into the elegant and refined Madeleine, as Scottie (comfortable and powerful) also remakes the vulgar Judy (twice over) into Madeleine, and both men, Elster and Scottie, lead the two women to a similar death of falling from the tower of the church at San Juan Batista, one death (of the real Madeleine) to appear as a suicide (Elster in fact had strangled his wife beforehand and thrown her from the tower), the other death (of Judy-Madeleine) like the death of the real Madeleine and equally ambiguous. It is not clear, for example, when Judy dies, if it was an accident (her taking fright) or purposeful (her taking her life). In any case, by then, Judy is effectively already fictionally dead (as Madeleine had really been dead), Judy having lost her identity (rejected as Judy by Scottie in order for him to resurrect her in the image of Madeleine). As Elster had done, that image is no more real than the image of Carlotta. Both are mocked by Hitchcock in the overlapped image of plain Madge in a painting of her clothed as Carlotta – an image of an image of an image – exactly as Judy is clothed as Madeleine. Madge loves Scottie as Judy does and like her is rejected by him for what she really is, that is, not in conformity to an image. The gestures of Elster and of Scottie at the top of the tower holding Madeleine-Judy are similar, but reversed, the one the true as false and the other the false as true, the one an image as a reality, the other reality as an image.

In the play of doubles and multiple fictions, place and time are crucial, since time repeats itself, finds its doubles (Carlotta to Madeleine to Judy to Kim Novak and, also, Carlotta's lover to Elster to Scottie to James Stewart). There is also the image of old San Francisco (its buildings and sites and its social conventions, notably, what rich and powerful men could then do to women in order to suit their desires) duplicated in the present San Francisco (by sites visited, by the likeness of clothing – Judy is perpetually in costume, in, if not fancy dress, false dress – by the theme-like park of San Juan Batista). The monastery of San Juan Batista is a replica of the monastery from the past, of time frozen, eternalised, made into the present, as Scottie sought to eternalise Madeleine, as he went from acrophobia to catatonia, to necrophobia. San Juan Batista is also the replica of a concocted dream which Madeleine-Judy fabricates to Scottie in order to lead him to the scene of the false suicide as she herself is a fabrication. The present is dressed as the past geographically, sexually, emotionally, erotically, as pure appearance, as an image, not exactly without substance but whose reality is elsewhere and perverted.

Fiction films by definition 'dress' realities: story is a fabrication. The constituents of the fabricated fiction include its characters, settings, objects (keys, bottles, spectacles, tea bags, a bunch of flowers, ink) costuming (with its accessories of scarves, stockings, necklaces, rings, handbags, gloves), also make-up, hairdo and the acting out of roles, in short, the make-believe, the artifice and theatricality that transform persons and things into the appearances of them, into pure surface, reality into its similitude, in short, into representations, into images, how things appear rather than what they are or might signify (often, in Hitchcock, nothing at all, a MacGuffin, a pretext, a mere and often unfounded suspicion, a guilty intent or projection). Film, in this guise of dress, of appearance and artifice, is an extension of the fashion industry, the playing out of roles by gesture, costume, imaginings and the provocation of desire (social, individual, sexual). Godard sees Hollywood as the embodiment of Max Factor.

Films create the double of reality in its images of it. Hitchcock takes doubling and resemblance to considerable lengths. His films are not only (as with most fiction films) a duplicate of reality (an illusion of it), but within his films and central to their narrative is duplication and the lure of imitation – that is, imitation, repetition and resemblance are its fictional motives; not only do his films create illusions for an audience, but within the films characters create for themselves stories and illusions that fuel the action and their emotions, indeed are the action and the story, the playing out of a fantasy upon reality; the transformation of the one by the other and then back again, when the film concludes and the fantasy resolved. The 'drama', the 'suspense' in Hitchcock's films is dependent upon doubling, hallucinations, simulations: the wrong man, false interpretations, a transfer of guilt, the ubiquity of crime, projections of desire. Every object is a sign, every sign a false lure: that is, the Hitchcock film doubles itself, presenting the spectator with a fiction (one that compels, that becomes for the viewer subjective, that creates desire, fright, apprehension, suspense), and also presents its characters with a similar situation, a make-believe that seems terrifyingly real; more precisely, his characters create their own fictions (interpretations) or are caught up in the fictions of others (suspicion, doubt, desire), enter from the everyday and the normal into the fictional and the extraordinary, even unbelievable, and so much so that the consequences can be deadly. (The real is never completely deserted by Hitchcock or by his characters, who, on the contrary, walk a thin line between what they observe and what they desire.) The audience, by identification, is doubled in the characters (they look, the spectator looks, the regards overlap, as in *Rear Window*). It is the reason why, perhaps, the spectator can be as much troubled and gripped by the fate of the villain (the more villainous, the more 'interested' the spectator becomes as in *Shadow of a Doubt, Strangers on a Train, Rope, Lifeboat*) as by the fate of the main character (usually innocent in fact but thought to be guilty in imagination which proves more powerful than fact). It is the form of this situation that catches the attention, that 'tells'.

Just as the audience enters a make-believe fantasy, is 'taken', literally possessed, led by its own desires and fears, and by a voyeurism at the spectacle of things, so too do the characters act similarly (they act out a role *and* are observers of their actions, as if to act is also to comment, *North by Northwest, I Confess* and *The Wrong Man* are perfect examples). In so doing, they serve as a mirror to the audience, and for that reason everything seen in a Hitchcock film appears to be true because it is represented visually and objectively and also is false because it is mistakenly interpreted. Hitchcock provokes the 'wrong' decision, the 'false' assessment of what he presents visually as rigorously true. Indeed, it is the gap on which his films depend and without it there could be no 'wrong', no 'reason'. The object for the characters becomes an image, a sign and thereby liable to be misunderstood. It is not the objects nor the situations that are false but their understanding that falsifies them. The 'wrong' man and the 'false' appearance are everywhere, everything divided and in movement between what is objective and what is subjectively regarded and projected. The two perspectives overlap and are forever in play, as if, to return to costuming and to figures like Mrs Smith or Marnie, or Grace Kelly in *Rear Window*, or Roger Thornhill, the clothes you wear, the fashion you adopt are both yourself and your image, who you are and what you project or are taken for, the murderer dressed as a priest in *I Confess*. Masquerade and mistaken identity are permanent features in Hitchcock's films.

Everything in his films is nothing if not deceptive (for the characters and with a delay or hiatus, for the audience). Interpretation and stories become everything while reality (sight) practically nothing at all. The price for misinterpretation can be severe: murder or attempted murder, death, or its risk. If in Hitchcock's films the image is always true – that is, is never faked (*Stagefright* again is the exception with its 'false' flashback) – it is the regard of what is that falsifies or is in error in judgement and awareness (the crop-dusting sequence in *North by Northwest*, initially the birds in *The Birds*); it is here I believe that there is a correlation between Hitchcock and Surrealism. (Scottie, the hard-nosed detective in *Vertigo*, believes the incredible tale of Gavin Elster about his wife being inhabited by spirits from the past because he wants to believe and he wants to because he is in love with the image of Madeleine – an impersonation – one that he sees and that traps him at Ernie's, a true image but a false understanding, pure reality and pure imagination, as in Breton's *Nadja*. *Vertigo* is the story of an *Amour fou*).

The characters not only tell themselves stories (as in *Suspicion* and *Notorious*) or believe stories told them (*Vertigo*, *The Man who Knew too Much*, *North by Northwest*) that send them on a quest – often on a pursuit – after nothing very substantial at all, no matter how impossible and unlikely these might be, they are caught, literally trapped by narratives based on appearance and fuelled by desire (real-seeming and objective, at the same time fanciful, projected, imaginary and subjective).

Eric Rohmer, who, with Claude Chabrol in the 1950s, wrote what is still the best analysis of Hitchcock's cinema, constructed in his own films an aesthetic of light comedy dependent on what is seen and what is said to have been seen (interpretation). His characters create a narrative in which they are the heroes and heroines on the basis of little beyond their own fantasies and imagination.

Practically nothing in a Hitchcock film is as it seems to be. Often events and objects are (as is the case in *Vertigo*) signifiers without a referent, empty signs full of misplaced drama and emotion, the terror and the comic irony in Hitchcock's films. Suspense for the audience involves the delayed resolution of the fiction in which the characters find themselves, the tear in the seamlessness and homogeneity of the ordinary, finally restored, a tear initiated by an entry into the fabricated but finally mended. When Carole Lombard in *Mr and Mrs Smith* tries to fit into the dress she wore when Mr Smith had first courted her in order for them to return to and re-enact the past (as in *Vertigo*), the dress comes away at the sides. It no longer fits her. Her body has grown out of it; there is no way back to the woman she once was and to the courtship and desire she had then experienced. She remarks that the dress has shrunk not that she had expanded as if her double from the past is unchanged in the present, her beauty and body intact and eternal while it is the world, she asserts, that has changed, circumstances, as in *Vertigo*, in its return by the characters to a San Francisco that once was whose reincarnation in the present goes awry – what is imagined no longer fits reality – the comedy in one film and death in the other. There is no way back.

It is stretching a point, I am sure, but the comedy and the tragedies of Hitchcock, especially his doomed heroines, belong to melodrama and perhaps most to Flaubert's *Madame Bovary*, Emma in love with the romances of literature, seeking, and with such dreadful consequences, to make reality into a dream, to transmute fact into fiction (as Flaubert does) and along the way impoverish herself and her husband in debts to the draper for bonnets, skirts, ribbons and gloves; her impoverishment and the pursuit of the insubstantial, of appearance and the fictional by her finery and the dreams they signify is the richness of the fiction.

Jacques Rivette

Jacques Rivette was a founder along with Éric Rohmer of the film journal *Gazette du cinéma* in 1950. He wrote for *Cahiers du cinéma* from its beginnings in the late 1950s as did other future film directors of the French Nouvelle Vague. From 1963 to 1965, Rivette was the editor-in-chief of Cahiers. If, as Godard argued, watching films and writing about them was a way to make films, the reverse was also true, namely that making films was a way to write about them, and critically. Every film made by the Nouvelle Vague directors was also an essay on the cinema and a response to André Bazin's question, *Qu'est-ce que le cinéma?*

It was customary at *Cahiers* to write about films and filmmakers that one admired. Among Rivette's most interesting and illuminating articles in *Cahiers* were those about Alfred Hitchcock, Howard Hawks, Roberto Rossellini and Jean Renoir. Almost all of Rivette's films, with varying emphases, pay tribute to these film-makers, especially to Renoir about whom Rivette made a documentary in 1966. His films were at once 'Renoirian', 'Rossellinian' and 'Hawksian'.

Like Rossellini, Rivette does not primarily rely on a script in the usual sense. He does depend on an outline, a rough sketch and synopsis, though nothing detailed: not dialogue, nor *découpage*, nor indications of how a scene was to be shot. Instead, often at the last minute, the evening before shooting or just before on the same day, Rivette would discuss with the actors and technicians how things might proceed, and at that point a script would be prepared and followed, often to the letter. On the one hand there was chance (anything could happen, possibilities were open) and on the other hand, tight control once a decision was made. The see-saw of freedom (openness, a refusal of control) and constraint (strict control) was a daily occurrence, but the constraint and the openness were not outside the film, exterior to it; as part of its production, but in the film as a crucial element of its structure and narrative. Once a film began to develop and a plot to take shape, it was the film that controlled things. Rivette's 'method' placed everything (the film) and everyone (cast, scriptwriter) at risk. His way of working was discomfiting since coherence was in jeopardy, pathways and outcomes made uncertain as if the film and all associated with it were brought toward an abyss; it was also reassuring, the reassurance of continuity, one event, shot, sequence leading to another as consequence, though not necessarily as causation.

The process of 'just before' and 'at the last minute' was repeated until the completion of the film. Rivette tended to regard a shot or a sequence less in terms of continuity, however, than as complete in itself – that is, continuity was established between autonomous units, self-contained narratives which the 'next' shot or sequence functioned less to complete than to complicate, to foster the possibility of sudden surprises and new encounters while at the same time tightening a grip on the film and its characters, as if freedom and choice *necessarily* led to their negation, to the opposite. The lesson and the model came from Hawks, a lucid, straightforward, linear continuity that nevertheless entangled and trapped characters precisely as they attempted to organise and order things to a achieve a satisfactory end (freedom, release), to resolve a predicament as in *Rio Bravo* (1958) or *Red River* (1948) or to find a way out of the situation they had created, by their organising. It was as if the labyrinth in which they found themselves and the obstacles they encountered were the consequence of actions (and of logic) designed for liberation. The Hawks model is striking for a 'modern' film, the films of Godard for example, where instead of continuity, there are fragments and instead of linearity, juxtapositions where plot and intrigue seem hardly to hold because the films lack the necessary homogeneity and coherence for these to succeed.

The writing of a Rivette film does not precede it, but is simultaneous with it. The films have an 'inside' (what is represented) and an 'outside' (the representing); Rivette made both 'visible'; indeed, their relation was *the* play, *the* theatre, since in addition to the story the film told, it told the story of its own telling and becoming, thus reflecting itself, like a mirror. In *Jeanne La Pucelle* (1997), for example, Jeanne seeks to enact her will, not despite the obstacles she encounters, but with their help, seizing opportunities as thrown up by chance and by being attentive and flexible. The film is in a similar situation, subject to the vagaries of weather, finance, costumes, lighting, sudden occurrences and insights, a casual gesture, all of which Rivette turns to good account, like Jeanne d'Arc does, even to the very end.

Rivette's method required that his films be shot in continuity so that what happened earlier would affect, indeed dictate, what would come later (a plot or the development of an intrigue) and thus at every point, the logic of the film would impose itself. By this process, the film was 'open' to possibilities, chance, accident, inspiration, in effect, perpetually in a state of 'becoming' not in accord with a prepared plan, but in accord with its own processes and rhythms as these were decided upon in their course of development and as they took shape, responsive to chance and inspiration. On the other hand, such 'openness' as it proceeds becomes a constraint, narrowing possibilities, testing (and risking) inspiration, invention, the instant.

Most films involve make-believe. Actors make believe they are characters, films make believe they are windows on reality, directors make believe they are in control and that the film is 'theirs'. Yet if the construction of reality is an aim, the fact of acting and of make-believe, indeed of construction, compromise it. To make believe that what is make-believe is true, that fiction is fact, is to establish a realm of the false as the reign of the true (a Renoirian lesson). When an actor becomes 'other' to him or to herself becoming a character that he or she 'plays', the consequence may be false (being other than you are), but the activity, the play, is never so: the 'true' actor 'truly' acts, artifice is real, stage and staging are palpable and concrete, the imposture made evident and is always true.

When, in a Rivette film, a plot takes shape and constrains, the actors respond to it and that response is their action and the 'play'. What is plotted may be false, but the response to it is not and the plot truly itself. Rivette's models (and Renoir's, for example, in his *La Carosse d'or*) are 'classical', of the eighteenth century: Marivaux, Beaumarchais and Mozart.

A film is false and true, true because it is false (acted, contrived, given a plot) and false when it is made to seem true (a verisimilitude). Some film-makers like Rivette and Renoir go to great lengths to stress the artificial and point to it. With Bresson, the 'cinema' is the residue when all that is not cinema (for him 'theatre') is stripped away; for Rivette the 'cinema' is more simply the structure of the play, the presence of the film and nothing is stripped away. It is a different notion of the 'pure'. The narrative remains as a force and a limit and is responded to and must be respected. The difference to Bresson is that in Rivette the presence of story, intrigue and plot are acknowledged, starred, reckoned with, brought into the open and put into action.

Rather than film serving to illustrate a subject or a drama, it is subject and drama that illuminate the film and its workings, its plot (and plotting), scheming, intrigue, in short, its artifice and theatre. What is 'true' in these films, to use an overworked term, is the *cinematic*, and it is a much broader and inclusive thing for Rivette than for minimalists like Bresson and Straub; the purity of the Rivette film involves staging, structuring, capturing, shooting; the grace of movements, gestures, harmonies, resonances, tonalities, rhythms, performances, not simply performances within the film, but the performance of the film, its dramatisations and theatricality.

Rivette, by leaving dialogue, the development of plot, reactions and gestures in performance (*mise en scène*) to the last minute while involving cast and crew in decisions as to how the film should proceed, preserves (as does Rossellini) a freshness and immediacy, along with the unexpected of the vagaries of chance since almost nothing of the details is known in advance. Such film-making preserves the gap (effaced in most films) between what is performed 'in scene' and the performance and putting into scene, the *mise en scène* that makes it visible, present. If one weeps at the performance of the Cancan in the magnificent finale of Renoir's *French Can Can* (1953), they are tears for colour, movement, joy and release what Nini had been willing to renounce before she consented to dance, for the sake of jealousies in the world, for the sake of reality, but once she is dancing, once in the film and performing on stage before an audience, nothing else matters. She is 'caught'. She loves what she does without reserve, enters it and the performance and the film completely, the spectacle is irresistible, even for Danglard. It is one of the great moments of cinema where there is nothing else but the Cancan, the stage, the girls, the colour, the evocation of a past made present and the joy of it.

The Rivettian 'method' establishes a dialogue internal to the film (as with the films of Renoir) between what the film represents and the representing of it, between the fiction and its creation, between control and freedom, and between the plot (its machinations) that determines, limits and imposes a logic, reduces possibilities (especially since shooting is in continuity) and yet allows for the unexpected, for surprise, and immediacy that may disrupt, may overturn constraint, in short, the difference between what is real-seeming, and fictional (false) and the 'truth' of the purely cinematographic.

In Rivette's films every attempt by the film and its characters to escape the necessities and constraints imposed on them by plot, constraints that in theory they are able to alter at any moment in the planning and course of the film, results instead in the constraints becoming all the more powerful as if the film once on the move and by the logic of its continuity was moving beyond control, and whose direction needed not only to be recognised but embraced.

Jeanne and the Historical Fiction

Neither Rivette nor the actors in *Jeanne la Pucelle*, including Sandrine Bonnaire who 'plays' Jeanne, have control over the outcome of the events in the film since these are known in advance, dictated by history: the siege of Orléans will be lifted, Charles will be crowned at Rheims, the Burgundians will capture Jeanne and sell her to the English, soldiers will attempt to rape her, Jeanne will confess, she will recant her 'confession' and she will be burned at the stake as a heretic, an apostate and a witch. History itself is a limit. Representations in a historical film represent a 'second time'. What has been before is made to occur again, the past re-enacted in the present by shadows and shades of history, characters who act, beings once substantial and now, in film, only characters, who, at best, resemble their originals, and while the original action is innocent as are the original historical figures (the innocence of the first time), the repetition of it in the present, that seeks to reinstate a past, is, necessarily, no longer innocent, but an imposture. In such circumstances of the historical and of re-enactment, it is difficult for any action not to fall into the false. The sign and skill of good classical acting is to make the false seem true – that is, for the second time to appear as the first time. What Rivette values is not the 'realism' of the nineteenth century (impersonations), but the artifice of the eighteenth and before that of *Commedia dell'arte*, of the clown, mountebank, acrobat, of the grotesque, of masquerade, of the circus, what Eisenstein presented in *Strike* and Chaplin and Keaton in their films.

In the process of making believe (the imposture) that

one is not oneself, but the other, the only thing 'true' is the imposture (Sandrine as Jeanne, Sandrine the player and the modern film, *Jeanne La Pucelle*, as the fifteenth-century past). Sandrine is present when Jeanne is and the contemporary is present when the action is fictively set 500 years in the past. The more real-seeming the film, the more dishonest it is, whereas a film that points to its artifice (the musical comedy is a perfect example as is the best of Renoir) is most honest by being purely cinema and true to itself. What so troubled the early avant-garde about the cinema was not its deceits, but the hiding of them ... a lack of honesty, their naturalism.

Central to the fiction of *Jeanne la Pucelle* is the issue of whether it can be believed that Jeanne is following the voices and commands of God and his angels: Saint Michel, Sainte Marguerite and Sainte Catherine who Jeanne says have visited her, or that Jeanne instead has invented a story of visions, asserting visitations that never took place, creating herself a figure of her own fiction, as occurs to the characters in Rohmer's films, Grace Elliot, for example, in *L'Anglaise et le duc* (2002), or as someone (sincerely) believing in fantasms, spectres, visions – in short, fictions – to be realities, but which are rather figments of imagination created by desires as happens in Hitchcock's films.

The issue is a constant in the film from its beginning: Jeanne needs to convince first the Captain of the French troops of her mission, then the Dauphin, then the clergy, then the army that she is genuine, that she is who she says she is, that she saw what she says she saw, and will accomplish what she wishes because God (in whom she and they believe) commands her. It is the manipulations at her trial by the judges that condemns her by 'proving' (to the satisfaction of the judges though decided in advance even before the trial) that she is not who or what she says she is, but an impostor. Such imposture and claims are heretical and as a heretic Jeanne must die, be cleansed in fire. God is her fiction, say those who judge her, and the Devil her truth though Jeanne believes herself to be innocent and pure as God is her witness. For her judges, Jeanne is acting – or worse, claiming – her act as sincere, claiming unreality and falsity as the real and the true. Crucial to the trial is her decision, toward the end of the trial, not to be truthful, to agree with her judges, because she is afraid to die and believes that the court will in its turn be lenient and therefore she admits her heresy to it (which is her lie), denying who she 'truly' is by, once again, dressing as a woman, denouncing her claim to Divine guidance and intimacy, thus denying that she has been telling the truth and therefore betraying herself and her faith. Then, after an attempted rape by British soldiers, and still in chains, she realises that she will never be free by renouncing her beliefs, and thus is 'forced', in order to be free, to 'recant', to deny her denial and therefore to accept her fate.

Every gesture and move toward liberation and victory by Jeanne, save her final recantation, confines her all the more. Behind every play and every action in her pursuit of freedom (for herself, for her soldiers, for France) is terror and imprisonment, a Rossellini lesson, the one he tells in *Stromboli* (1950), *Europa '51* (1952) and *Il Messia* (1976) . The issue for Jeanne, to save her body by losing her soul, or saving her soul by sacrificing her body, is a theme of the film, essentially unresolvable and paradoxical since by freeing one part, she loses the other. In the end, she must choose. War, for example, is a spiritual necessity (commanded by God and the angels and a metaphor for struggle) and physical risk (to be pierced by arrows, threatened by pain, torture and death. If Jeanne is an impostor, as the judges assert, her actions, military (to fight) and spiritual (to pray) would only be theatre, a game, acting, fraudulence, not as claims, purity and piety, certainly not innocence. To 'act' is the reverse of innocence.

For her captors it was important to demonstrate that Jeanne was indeed guilty and that her testimony was false and thereby her claim made her a heretic since her imposture would make illegitimate the principal theatrical event in the film – the crowning of the Dauphin at Rheims – as only theatre, politics, reasons of State, corrupt not spiritual, all the more despicable for the magnificence of its *mise en scène*, the ceremony of the sacred at the coronation in the service of power not faith, mirrored exactly by the clergy in their trial of Jeanne the trial about religion and sanctity, a masquerade in the exercise in political power.

What occurs therefore 'in' the film, 'within' its representations, is an echo of the play 'of' the film whose second time, whose repetition of innocence (real action), is pure theatre and in being so, in being repetition, becomes purely cinema. Film as representation is always a repetition, a recording, a second time. It is never innocent (as Hitchcock demonstrates) and therefore for Rivette and for Hitchcock, the truth is not the subject nor the story, but their creation, the artifice of plot, labyrinth, falsities, concealment, injustice, in effect, the film. The falsity of film (the assertion of a realism), its negativity (its denial of artifice), its unresolved paradox (true when it is most false, false when it insists it is true), is forever on trial for its apparent purity of intentions. That is, what is the game in the film is not Jeanne's truth or heroism or even her life, but the existence and truth of the film as it weaves around the line that separates play and reality, freedom and control and Jeanne's refusal to recant. The film repeats theatre, repeats history, repeats reality, in the play of its intrigues between freedom and terror.

No more with Rivette than with Renoir, are life and theatre or life and film at odds, in opposition, though neither are they the same thing. What is involved instead is the movement and shift between, one that obscures borders and the definite, that muddies difference, makes possible an intermingling (what Pasolini would call contamination) and declares the paradox.

It is important for the truth of the film, that Jeanne's visions are testified to as realities of vision, and equally important that the shadows produced by the film (characters, châteaux, fortresses, ceremonies, events), the figures that it sets into motion are also true, but as visions and plot.

Power

In Rivette's films, as in his *Jeanne la Pucelle*, it is women who create stories by their words and men (soldiers, judges, kings) who deny the truth of them by asserting 'reality' against stories and against the tellers ('only a woman', a 'whore'). Hence, the women, Jeanne in this film, are forced to deny the denial made against them and the denial of them, to reject their rejection, to negate power, not by words (these have already been discounted), but by deeds, by making visible (dressing as a man, killing, making words come true, choosing the stake as an affirmation against power, being a soldier), demonstrating the powerlessness of power. In the end, it is her judges who are impotent and Jeanne triumphant. Jeanne, dressed as a man, her hair shorn, is more herself than when she had long hair and dressed in feminine robes. Now as opposed to then she is acting like a man is 'among' men, among brothers. It is impossible not to think of Hawks in this context, his 'masculine' women and of men cross-dressing. The strangest, most odd and uncomfortable scenes in the film are when Jeanne is among women, dressed as a woman and thereby least herself.

What Jeanne does, the film does – that is, 'makes visible', 'brings back' – what has been forgotten in the image and forgotten by history and reason: angels, shadows, sanctity, truth, the lost and all that which power has excluded, backed by its claim of reality (women, the peripheral, the out-of-focus, the invisible, the fantastic and the enchanting). Rivette's films are always on the side of women, not because they might be identified with unreality, but, to the contrary.

Duration

One purpose of 'the last minute' is not only to leave a space for the unexpected, for the accidental and for surprise to make its appearance, to be given a chance, to be able to improvise, but also (and perhaps most of all) to make possible encounters with what is absent, what the film contains but cannot yet be seen, as if these are buried, themes of all Rivette's films without exception and in some films, glaringly so, for example *La Religeuse* (1966), *Céline et Julie vont en bateau* (1974), *La Belle noiseuse* (1990), *Va Savoir* (2001) – a theatre of the hidden, the purloined and of sudden discoveries and revelations and not of truth but of the plot.

Rivette's films become by that fact archaeological, and what they bring to light, into light, to the surface, and the visible, is another film or films, pathways and alternative narratives within the film, after Rossellini, for example, as in his *Viaggio in Italia* (1954), *Generale della Rovere* (1959). The Rivette film, then, is less representation than an experiment with film, something tentative, searching, a discovery and an encounter, above all alive. What is discovered and met is always multiple, never closed, and however tight the knots of the plot, more a matter of density than conclusion or resolution.

What is important about the second time, the repetition and that appears at the last moment (instantaneous and a surprise) is the opportunity it gives to re-examine what had been not representational truth but cinematic structure, mechanism, that is to say the archaeology of the second time is above all analytical, a taking-apart of forms by the asking of questions in order to see how things work (worked) as one might dismantle a clock, and not only to discover how the original (the historical, the innocent) may have worked, but the mechanism of the second time, the yield of dismantling, destructuring, reconstructing. Effectively, what lies buried and beneath the surface of representations are the mechanisms and forms that have brought them into being, that gave them existence and ushered in the second time. *Jeanne la Pucelle* is not only a historical narrative, but the revelation of what makes it so, the conditions and theatre and *mise en scène* that Rivette, with the help of Sandrine Bonnaire, brings to view. The story of *Jeanne la Pucelle* is the story less of her life than the life of a film. It is what the film uncovers and reveals. Because there is much that lies buried and nothing is quite as it appears to be in this film (all his films) of journey, intrigue and encounters does Rivette feel he has no right to repress or make invisible, to lose once again what had been previously lost and face the dilemma then of choice to select this and reject that as the film turns and whose turning we view. Rivette's entire effort in the cinema is in the other direction. Not only is the spirit of the cinema refound by Rivette (a lesson of the *Nouvelle Vague*) but, of necessity, so too is the body of the film (its duration, time, the ordering of spaces and objects, the *mise en scène*) which is extended, expanded, fleshed out, given presence, as if there is no end to the cinema, no finality to the play of the real and the fictions to which it gives birth and the artifice it requires in order to remain true. Hence the great length of his films, yet their essential brevity as if taking place in a flash, confounding time. Nothing less would have done.

1 *Judex*, Louis Feuillade

2 *Science in fiction, the sea horse*, Jean Painlevé

3 *L'Atalante*, Jean Vigo

4 *L'Atalante*, Jean Vigo

5 *Blood of the Beast*, Georges Franju

6 *Playtime*, Jacques Tati

7 *La Vie moderne*, Raymond Depardon

8 *Vertigo*, Alfred Hitchcock

9 *Jeanne la Pucelle I – Les batailles*, Jacques Rivette

10 *Histoire(s) du cinéma*, Jean-Luc Godard

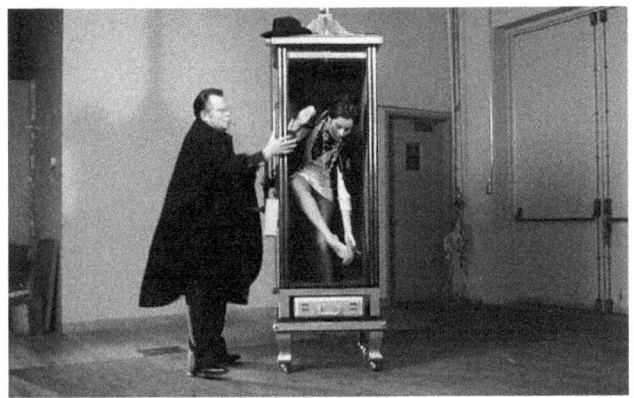

11 *F for Fake*, Orson Welles

12 *Man of the West*, Anthony Mann

13 *La terra trema*, Luchino Visconti

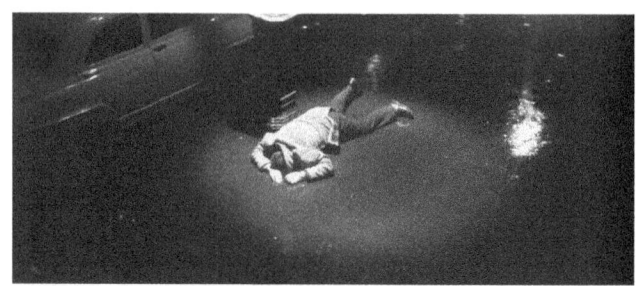

14 *Shoot the Piano Player*, François Truffaut

15 *She Wore a Yellow Ribbon*, John Ford

Jean-Luc Godard

(the) Frame

Godard's exhibition at the Centre Pompidou in Paris, *Voyage(s) en Utopie, Jean-Luc Godard, 1946–2006: À la recherche d'un théorème perdu*, was in three rooms each consisting of a number of installations and a collection of objects at first sight seemingly set out higgledy piggledy. It was as if each room constituted in itself an installation. As with his *Histoire(s) du cinéma* the materials were either cited (images, sounds, phrases), found (a bed, a broom, steps, a model electric train), or reconstructed and miniaturised (the *maquette* of the unrealised original exhibition for the Pompidou, *Collages de France*). These various materials from different provenances were brought together as in a super collage (the entire exhibit), not exactly a parody, but certainly a commentary on traditional museum classifications by genre, artist, period, nationality. The disjunctions between what was displayed – because of the apparent arbitrariness and the unfamiliarity of the joins (not unlike Surrealist experiments from the 1930s) – provoked memories, associations and surprising unlikely connections. For example, the toy electric train that ran in a loop through a tunnel variously seemed to cite Hitchcock's *North by Northwest* (1959), the Lumière brothers' *L'Arrivée d'un train en gare di Ciotat* (1895), Orson Welles's ecstatic comment on the studio machinery offered him at RKO for *Citizen Kane*

(1941) – 'This is the biggest electric train set any boy ever had!' and, as well, the trains that transported the victims of the Holocaust to Auschwitz and Bergen-Belsen, images which Godard earlier had reproduced in his *Histoire(s) du cinéma*, some taken from Alain Resnais's *Nuit et brouillard*, others from George Steven's home movie that ends with his entry into the death camps just after D-Day, others from Claude Lanzmann's *Shoah* (1985) and still others that were archival. Some of the material, such as the *Collages de France* miniature (like a model for a film set), was reduced in size and projected (looped on flat small screens of fragments from films by Godard and others: Nicholas Ray, Sergei Eisenstein, Otto Preminger, placed alongside anonymous pornographic images and those from sport), an odd collection, as you might find in a junk shop and be provoked by to dream and imagine, to be transported.

Though objects and associations tended to coalesce on contact, they also tended to disperse, going off in different directions to their origins and beyond, making of the exhibition a map of pathways and possible journeys that exceeded it, defying any presumed unity. No one thing sufficed, each was particular (none 'served' an apparent function) and all were plural because they suggested multiple places and entries.

The exhibition, because of its apparent disorder, citational density, heterogeneity, evocations and the banality of the collection of its found objects, echoed works of Dada, particularly Kurt Schwitters's *Merzbau*, and of the common objects, or odd conjunctions some scandalous, displayed by Marcel Duchamp (his urinal, for example and the moustache on the *Mona Lisa*). It also resonated with the Combines and installation pieces of Robert Rauschenberg which in turn echoed strategies in Cubist collages, those of Picasso, for example, and before Picasso, the purified, almost abstract, sculpted and geometric paintings of Paul Cézanne. There was as well an echo of the Surrealists, their art works, literary works, and films, not only the Buñuel-Dali films and their improbable juxtapositions, but also Joseph Cornell's film, *Rose Hobart* (1936), a remake/citation of *East of Borneo* (1931), like the Pompidou exhibit and Godard's *Histoire(s) du cinéma*.

It was the 'reality' and everydayness of things in the exhibition, as if 'documents' of the real, also true of the cited images and sounds of *Histoire(s) du cinéma* whose organisation and connections are often as obscure as these are in the exhibition, that are disorienting by the fact of their 'reality', the lack of any single precise narrative or 'line' to contain them and their resistance to 'sense'. The 'real' and its contrary multiple openings to possible other arrangements and references, including an opening to fictions not-yet-formed or articulated (in *Histoire(s)* to films that 'might be'), is disruptive of any unified coherence while the dailiness and casualness, the sense of chance encounters between different materials (as in Surrealist *rencontres*) gave the exhibition and *Histoire(s)* a sense of travelling (*voyage*), a wandering within an indeterminate geography without guidance or precise purpose or destination. It is not exactly Godard who is the *flâneur* but rather the film that almost seems as alive and palpable as a person.

The earliest drafts of *Histoire(s) du cinéma*, based on lectures given by Godard at the Montréal Cinémathèque in 1978, were divided into twelve voyages. The title of the Pompidou exhibition was *Voyage(s) en Utopie*, multiple wanderings to nowhere very exact, a vagabondage of memories, chance and an expectation-readiness for occurrences that might happen. These works are exciting, wonderful and open precisely because nothing definitive can be deduced. They are also uncomfortable for their apparent chaos and fortuity, their refusal to arrive or to come, like being lost.

Cubist collages not only recruited fragments excised from reality, as the Godard exhibition did, and mixed them together with paint and graphic lines (as in a 'painting'), but they did so as to compromise the traditional two dimensions of painting which historically had created a third dimension by the use of perspective: that is, an illusory one at the interior of a painted scene whose model was theatrical and dependent upon a strict respect for framing. The fact that these works recruited real objects constituted an intrusion into an imaginary, essentially fictionalised, representational space which the real compromised simply by its alien presence, as the will toward abstraction in Cézanne, pared down as it was, disturbed a prevailing naturalism, still evident in Impressionism. It too presented a new, 'other' note in a heretofore homogeneous space. What had been traditional was now confronted with radical differences (abstraction, the actual, the found, commentary, a remaking which was disruptive and parodic, signs of reordering that were neither beautiful nor even 'skillful' but instead questioning as different forms of questions and as questions of forms, articulated by Nicole Brenez in her 'The Forms of the Question').[1]

The Cubist collage created discontinuities (gaps) between the various items 'in' the collage and, by the addition of real material (cloth, wood, feathers, toys, matchboxes, newspaper clippings rather like the miniature boxes of scenes and objects in the work of Joseph Cornell), nor was there any glue (continuities) to hold these differences together. The Cubist work moved beyond its pictorial boundaries to an exterior third dimension (as opposed to a traditional illusory one interiorised within a frame by perspective, *trompe l'oeil*, and by a carefully wrought scenic composition). The actual 'third' dimension in the Cubist collage brings the exhibited work (like a painting) toward sculpture (cut-outs) and later what would be installations. The Cubist collage, because of its mix of materials (paper, wood, metal), its straining beyond the boundaries of the work and its resonance with the origins from which real objects that constituted had come or could be associated with, seems unfinished and infinite, in part for the fact that the frame had been traversed, focus endangered and thus painting, as it traditionally was, put at risk. For Picasso, it seemed that anything could become a subject for a work, could be a starting point. It was making do, an improvisation, the creation and transformation with whatever happened to be around, no object having a necessary permanence or definiteness, no reality thereby stable.

The collage was perpetually going away, going 'off', away from itself, beyond the framed limits that had been crucial for creating the illusionary scenes and figures of traditional painting, that had framed beauty and indicated skill. Even Picasso's purely painted canvasses seemed to be like cut-outs not because of their diverse materials (everything in those paintings is paint) so much as by its diverse and overlapping-intersecting volumes. The Cubist 'scene' not only lacked a fixed perspective and point of view, but was not, strictly speaking, representational and where it was, it approached parody. It did not describe, narrate or illustrate. Instead, it demonstrated (and sometimes cited).

Francis Bacon's work is also interesting in this regard. Bacon's frames rather than being traversed toward an outside beyond them, have the effect of constraining their subjects, tearing them apart by placing them under extreme pressure as if the painting and everything represented within it was about to explode and disintegrate and along with it the fact and idea of representation itself, its fragility and temporariness. Certainly, the frame rather than being a frame of perspective, depth and clarification tended toward so extreme a distortion that whatever was represented became purely form, shape, paint, rhythm, imbalance, as if the painting were dissolved into the pureness (chastity) of its constituents at the price of the coherence, stability or focus of any subject, as occurs with Picasso's art.

The installation work, Rauschenberg's *Combines*, Schwitter's *Merzbau* are the heirs to Cubist experiments and innovations and the revolution in painting it had initiated. A number of things were accomplished: the frame was discarded, the anecdotal narrative-theatrical scene dissolved, points of view multiplied, the centre destroyed, heterogeneity of material put into play and completeness and originality compromised. The consistencies and homogeneities characteristic of painting were made inconsistent and its unities (scenes) shattered into fragments by disjunctions in matter, temporality and dimension. These works spilled over boundaries and definitions that might contain or fix them, exceeding not only the practices but the categories, understandings, ideas, discourses and criticism that had served to define the artwork: frame, centre, point of view, perspective, description, meaning, significance, originality, beauty and sometimes narrative. As a result, what had previously simply been accepted and enjoyed for its skill and beauty and had given comfort by its sense (the represented, the anecdote, the piece of theatre) was now open to question ('what is art?'), to doubt and to uncertainty that went to the heart of the traditional artwork (pierced it) and its institutions as Duchamp's urinal and Warhol's Brillo Boxes and serialised images later provocatively made clear as if such questioning was one of, if not *the*, principal purpose of the artistic strategies of Surrealism, Dada and later their heir, Pop.

Godard's films in general and *Histoire(s) du cinéma* in particular, and evident in the Pompidou exhibition, echoed these accomplishments, especially the use of the artwork to bring itself into question and by extension all art where the work and the commentary upon it as in *Une Femme est une femme* (1961) – 'a musical and the idea of a musical' – were brought together thus making every element, image, sound concrete and discursive, representational and critical, focused and digressive. One of the achievements of *Histoire(s) du cinéma* is to so isolate images or sounds that these are refreshed, like seeing or hearing them anew and for the first time, no longer part of their origins nor immediately 'connected' to what surrounds them or is contiguous to them, and by so doing, by giving back to images, sounds, objects their autonomy, it freed them for any number of associations and encounters, none of which would cause them to lose their identity, as a continuous narrative might by restricting movement into fixed directions, by holding elements in place. In this multiplication of identities and possibilities nothing is lost and what has been can be seen once more (returns, memories), but differently, newly, for example Ethan Edwards taking Debbie in his arms in *The Searchers* (1956), fragmented, pulverised, retimed, broken down in *Histoire(s)*, but with nothing destroyed – to the contrary, enabling one (almost for the first time) to see the scene (because remade differently) and to bring it into a relation with other scenes elsewhere as if the function of *Histoire(s)* is not only for the film to be open and ready (attentive as in Rossellini's cinema) but to open up the cinema in general and in its details.

Historically, the questioning of the cinema – what it was, what it could become – an act of criticism and therefore necessarily a historical undertaking, had been the achievement of the films of the *Nouvelle Vague*, of its reflections on film in *Cahiers du cinéma* in the 1950s and 1960s, and coincident with both, perhaps even their source, certainly their inspiration, the writings of André Bazin and his philosophical pursuit of the cinema, *Qu'est ce que le cinéma?*, which made of films and their forms instruments of thought, giving them thereby an unaccustomed and extraordinary range and density.

In film, the frame has been defined by three interrelated aspects – the frame of the shot, the frame of the narrative which it served (a beginning and an end) and the continuities between shots that established scenes and sequences within a narrative to provide not only coherence and unity, a focus, but fictionality as a constructed simulacrum of the real. In other words, the frame(s) in film, as it had functioned in painting (and in theatre), was to contribute to the construction of an ideal illusory space within which a scene could be described, enacted and performed.

The frame was functional for narrative and therefore crucial to it. The destruction of the frame or at the very least compromising it, a deframing (the *Nouvelle Vague* was central in this process), affected an entire range of practices, ideas and histories where film and the commentary on film, contemporary film and the historical past of film were no more distinct nor distant than was fiction to documentary, precisely because borders were crossed and separations interconnected. One of the virtues of Godard was to bring into doubt categories and their (false?) oppositions, in order to begin to bring together what had been apart and in doing so propose differences as disjunctions that worked upon and with each other, active rather than fixed, in movement rather than locked in place and classified. This freedom (almost casual and instinctive, like the freedom and curiosity evoked in Surrealist encounters) and the intensity of play involved are the reason that Godard's films are so exhilarating.

Histoire(s) du cinéma accomplishes a massive deframing of the cinema and in doing so initiates a new history while not exactly closing a previous one, as *cleansing* it, as Cézanne cleansed painting. The traditional history of the cinema has been presented chronologically (a progressive narrative) where each film or group of films cited is made to belong to some kind of order, that is, the cited work as exemplary and illustrative (the 'silent' period, neorealism, the *Nouvelle Vague*, national cinemas, realism, formalism and so on), part of a classification system where every film represents and illustrates the history of the cinema and can be accounted for (counted). Such a history *typifies*. What *Histoire(s)* cleanses from the history of the cinema (and therefore from its practices) is the *typical*. The citation in Godard is a form that acts, one of whose functions is to disturb and dismantle every order. His *Histoire(s)* is, unlike most histories and stories, no longer dependent on structures of reference and direction or a narrative – that is, on a frame.

Narrative

Most Histories (*Histoires*), most histories of the cinema (*histoires du cinéma*) and most of the films that form part of that history and that tell stories (*histoires*) are narratives. They narrate events that have already occurred. The events so narrated are usually presented chronologically, a series of sequences, scenes, shots that progress in a more or less linear fashion, that begin and then are concluded. One of the features of such narratives is that their elements belong to a hierarchy of importance and significance. Some passages are strong, others weak, some dominant, others merely transitional or intermediary like punctuations in a succession.

Narrative itself is the consequence of a historical situation largely codified in the nineteenth century in the novel and in History writing, though also in painting and in theatre, and after the turn of that century, in film. Godard's films, from his first to his most recent, dismantle that tradition. His work is less a rejection of narrative as it had been practised (and largely still is) as it is a fragmentation and reordering of it, subjected to insistent interruptions, like a bell sounding or a telephone ringing in its midst.

In a Godard film, interruptions are not less important than what is interrupted, indeed the distinction between major and minor, representation and punctuation, *the* narrative and digressions from it, have little sense. All elements are equal (equally forms) and there is no classification system with all that implies of order and illustration. If his films, and especially his *Histoire(s) du cinéma*, are dense with citations and examples from the past, these are more like a collection or artistic options than a museum or archive ordered by fictions of classification. The combination of the indifference of elements to hierarchy, their resistance to a fixed order and place and their apparent equality in Godard's work establishes each element as autonomous and particular and also as available for rearrangement, hence the instability, circularity and sense of possibility in his films, their lack of finish and their energetic ceaselessness, porosity and meandering and thereby also the problem of speaking about them. How do you get hold of, begin to possess, a Godard work which is so unfixed and opaque?

What had been crucial to narrative – its coherence, unity, homogeneity, linearity, continuity, sense and order – are, in Godard's work, broken apart, constantly intruded upon. The citations that compose his films – overwhelming in *Histoire(s) du cinéma* – arrive from elsewhere such that the films are always moving away toward not only from where its elements originated but into new combinations and encounters with other elements, other citations. The narrative (if it had ever existed) is consumed by such movement. Alternative arrangements created by the unorthodox and plural succession of materials are not connected as linear motivated consequences. They are simply and merely successive. Their true place is not limited, but depends on encounters difficult to state or foresee and these are often simultaneous (the superimposition, fade, mix), disrupting time, or nearly so (rapid alternations, the flicker).

Most narratives, the grand narratives of History (*Histoire*) and the smaller histories (*histoires*), the stories and anecdotes they may contain, integrate the two. For example, to better understand Greek classical architecture, the political and social context of fifth-century Athens under Pericles might be discussed and the contrary, the political history of Athens might be illuminated by a detour through its architecture and sculpture. Similarly, the forms of the American cinema in the 1930s might be incorporated into a history of the studio system, a discussion of the films of John Ford or an analysis of the great Depression and the coming of sound to films. In these instances, the differences of Hollywood, the Depression, the studio system, John Ford, economy, ideology and art are grouped together within a homogeneous historical time with a foreground and background, the significant and less significant, marked lines of dependence and subordination. There is another way, that of associations (thematic, formal, remembrances) between discontinuous elements in sheets or layers of heterogeneous time and substance, as in for example André Malraux's *Le Musée imaginaire*, Walter Benjamin's *Arcade Project*, Aby Warburg's *Mnémosyne* and Godard's *Histoire(s) du cinéma*, collage-montages of non-contiguous and non-continuous fragments (citations), networks of echoes, resonances, rhythms, colours and space, that are like memories, or like pieces of music, in any case nothing definite or fixed, encounters which bear upon the present, that suddenly appear and give witness.

In *Histoire(s) du cinéma*, general history (wars, battles, economic arrangements, philosophical writings, the Holocaust, Hitler speaking, always a mixed bag), the history of the cinema (the films of the Soviet Union in the 1920s, Chaplin, the Nouvelle Vague, Italian neorealism, the studio system under Irving Thalberg) and the stories (*histoires*) of films evoked by cited fragments (from *The Searchers, M, Ordet, Potemkin, Broken Blossoms, La Règle du jeu, Cries and Whispers, Gigi, Paisà*), the history of art (Van Gogh, Picasso, Goya, Rembrandt, Utrillo, Matisse, pornography), all notable for their range, differences and distance from each other, are criss-crossed, made to intersect. They are not coordinated in the film, but rather overlap, are superimposed, flickered, appearing as simultaneous and distant, autonomous and, in counterpoint like a musical composition, they become form. Taken together, they do not 'explain', but rather 'explode', act, break open. They are dissonances that may coalesce or separate, forever being redrawn and not just occasionally, but constantly as new things are met and discovered. Godard brings things together not to explicate but to activate.

What is presented is a field of ceaseless movement and intersections where narrative and time are opened up. They are not exactly lost, but reconfigured as part of a composition, but not a narrative, nor a history, nor illustrations in the usual sense. The different cited histories, temporalities and instances that are brought into contact become multiple points of view, entries, appearances and disappearances, histories but not a history, documents but not a documentary. They are citations that illustrate nothing, but simply point. The fragments of histories, ruins of history and of narratives gathered in *Histoire(s)* work and interact to form not a new narrative and certainly not a new history. The history of the cinema as a narrative of narratives ceases to be sustainable.

Images of reality

All the images and scenes in *Histoire(s) du cinéma* are citations. If their origins cannot be found, it is certain, nevertheless, that in time they will be. Some scenes in the film are staged, for example monologues by professional actors: Alain Cuny, Sabine Azema, Julie Delpy, Juliette Binoche and Godard. The monologues are quotations from philosophy and poetry either directly or in a collage of phrases from different sources.

There is, I think, an argument in *Histoire(s)* or allusions to one, that historically the cinema did not realise its true potential of registering the real (this is the History of *Histoire(s)*). For example, it failed (except in rare instances) to foresee or engage with the horrors of war, the death camps or Sarajevo. For Godard, it seems, this failure has to do with a history of film as a history of narratives – that is, as illusion, a verisimilitude enacted by means of continuities and motivated connections. Thus, to reinstate the real to the cinema, *requires* the dissolution and break-up of narrative that *Histoire(s) du cinéma* accomplishes, not simply of little narratives but the grand narrative of History and the narrative in between, the history of the cinema. The dismemberment is the work of citation (extraction from a context, some kind of narrative) and montage (a recombination of forms).

French Impressionism, even if it had precedents in an earlier history of painting, created images out of doors, *en plein air*, in touch with the direct experience of nature, not an idealised view, but an actual one, the immediacy of the sketch, in order to capture the effects of light and mood, not eternal or immobile or idealised but found, encountered, if not exactly in a moment of time, within time in an actual present and in the reality of its passing. The paintings of Impressionism mark out temporality and the subjectivity necessarily attached to it in the capturing of an instant (like a photograph). What comes after Impressionism – Manet, Matisse, Cézanne, Picasso – is less an attempt to capture the real (though it is that too) than, as Foucault has pointed out,[2] to create paintings for the museum, paintings related to other paintings, to forms and hence freed from reproductive demands, demands that photography, and later film, would better satisfy. What occurred was not an either/or, either reality or artifice, reality or abstraction, but rather a play between the two, and hence an awareness of both at the heart of painting so that in being in the one place (of experience, of reality) necessarily led to the other (the image, consciousness), as with Godard's comment (and practice) whereby the document becomes fiction and fiction the document, neither stable and together, less an opposition than a difficult to define difference because of their closeness.

Disaffection toward narrative fiction or more precisely the felt need to question it belonged to a historical necessity. The film documentaries of the late 1920s and 1930s were in part provoked by political and social events which it was felt the fiction film did not adequately address (if at all) and because it was fiction and hence had excluded, for the sake of the coherence and effectiveness of its fictions, the real. However defined, the real was clearly a disturbance if brought within a highly organised, coded and institutionalised fictional practice. The forms of narrative fiction, if not threatened early on in the history of the cinema, were certainly called into question, the result of which (Renoir's films in this regard are exemplary) was a cinema that juxtaposed the real alongside the fictional or theatrical, the everyday and incidental beside eternal (beauty), that is as something 'other'. There were also documentaries which veered off into the fabulous and dreamlike at once under the spell of reality and aware of the subjectivity and hence magic and wonder and possibility (flexibility) within it (Vigo, Buñuel, Franju, Painlevé).

Given the fact that all of Godard's images and sounds in *Histoire(s) du cinéma* are cited (he is dealing with 'history', with the past), his material is necessarily second-hand, is already images. There are no images in the film of direct experience, no 'real' in the usual documentary sense of the real, no Eskimos hunting seal, except perhaps as memories, that is as already having been fashioned and which Godard can only 'cite' and 'remake'.

If the real is impossible to attain, why accuse the cinema of having betrayed its nature and vocation to register it? And why accuse it of failing to confront the actuality and horror of historical events? The problem for Godard is not that narrative fiction is fictional, but rather that it created an illusion as if it were not fictional but like life, as History-writing created false continuities and homogeneities as if true. The force of Godard's cinema and the work of his montage are to break up anything that immobilises and certifies including, or above all, an answer or strict determined oppositions. The real is not an object, but a relationship or, better, relationships, *Histoire(s)*, History with an 's', that fluctuates and is constantly subject to being reconfigured and at every (historical) moment. Nothing for Godard stands still, least of all his films. At best, the real can only be glimpsed, momentarily, in the in-between of perpetual rearrangements. It has no fixity any more than the past has, always subject to the vagaries of a present, to reconsiderations, to time, memory and the moment, no better demonstrated than Godard's reinstatement of the past in the future by the activity of his citations and their montage that causes what comes 'after', the next shot, to be what the present resurrects from the past, a transformed future as if the film is moving backward snatching the past, exhuming and projecting it forward. It involves an extended temporality like that which belongs to memory, reflection and thought.

In no sense, however, does *Histoire(s)* unfold time by means of events, but rather it points to time as an element of the shot and thereby makes everything ephemeral, always on the verge of disappearance, all the more so by the fact that the shot is an already pre-existing image, a citation, and thereby it is a return summoned by the present whose future is behind it and every shot belonging to multiple temporalities and directions.

Writing

It is difficult if not impossible to know how *Histoire(s) du cinéma* was made. Certainly it is not a film in the ordinary way which follows a plan, still less a script, not at all a story or a narrative and it is hardly an essay, and it destroys most systems of reference in the usual sense. What then determines not simply the images and sounds that appear but their relations to each other? Much of these seem illogical, undirected and, though it is possible sometimes to perceive an association, for the most part these are extremely distant and obscure even if these remote elements 'suddenly' fuse and coalesce. The film is not a representation but a manifestation, a demonstration (but of what?), a collection of documents whose order can be stated but whose significance is hard to discern. Above all, the film seems to be a record of the direct experience of making the film itself, an immediacy which results in an abundance of metaphors and signs but outside of the logical or the significant, even beyond control as if the film, in the instantaneities of its associations and linkages, has *written* itself.

Every film reconstitutes reality into signs – that is, the real is made into writing – thus leading to two kinds of critical discourse in part dependent on the way in which the film works: the relation of signs to the real (often as a simulacrum, a verisimilitude) and the relation of signs to each other, film as a way of thinking, like a language, but not this or that thought in particular. In *Histoire(s)* these signs in images and sounds are almost never direct, are already signs, already writing (films, literature, painting, music) – that is, citations, carrying with them resonances and meanings from a prior origin. The signs then are ready-mades, like Warhol's recasting, serialising images of Marilyn Monroe, or the objects long since discarded, now useless, functionless, that Rauschenberg brings together in his *Combines* made of strikingly oddly placed left-overs, brought back to life, absorbed into language, functioning as form, the real as writing but establishing nothing but that (already a great deal), film as discursive.

Histoire(s) then is a vast undertaking of remaking, repositioning, restating the already written. In doing so, it dismantles a functional writing. It de-writes, breaks logical connectives that gives writing back to film and makes film an instrument. Whatever is in the film is concretely itself (because disconnected, extracted, literally excavated) and at the same time potentially, like a word or sound or better yet, a phoneme, an independent unit on its own to serve within elsewheres, to be transferred and reused, resurrected, sent off on a myriad of pathways. Not any longer a scene in a narrative but a tool for creating a discourse. In that sense, these signs are indeed empty (potential) and this emptiness is their possibility, like a phoneme, a not-yet sign but the material for an infinite number.

Most films are written first in stages (the treatment, the script, the shooting script), then filmed, with the filming, the images being essentially an illustration of the writing (the writing come to life as visible scenes) and its effacement (the images cover-over the writing which has been written in order to disappear which is what a script is, a writing never to be fully realised as writing but only as a provisional plan or outline for filming). It is precisely the traditional role of the script with its apparent subordination of filming to the primacy of the word (and of literature) that Godard explicitly challenges in *Histoire(s)* not only by direct statements and cited examples, but in practice, converting images and sounds into an autonomous *writing*, film as writing, the experience of it and thereby a different kind of primacy. If traditional writing *for* film was self-effacing, Godard's writing *with* film is declamatory. The first kind of writing constructed a make-believe and thus it was forced to hide. Godard's writing is a dialogue with the real and thus must be evident. It is the very purpose and project of his film. The writing has two related practices. There are actual words projected, written and spoken (words become images) and then dismantled, to function as provocations, anagrams, elisions, opacity, the source of new words, phrases, images, signs all jumbled, their elements dispersed, then reworded, reassigned, coming together differently. The other practice involves the conversion (a transfer, relocation) of images and sounds into constituents of signs so that they are a writing, not to represent or signify, but to be manifest, demonstrative.

Notes

1 Brenez 2004, pp. 160–77.
2 See in this regard Badiou 1998, p. 86; Godard and Ishaghpour 2000, p. 43; Didi-Huberman 2003, p. 128.

Orson Welles

Citizen Kane

Orson Welles was born in 1915 in Kenosha Wisconsin. By all accounts he was a child prodigy, energetic, inventive, interested in spectacle and magic. In his late teens, at the beginning of the 1930s, he became involved in theatre. During the 1930s depression and the Presidency of Franklin Delano Roosevelt, Welles joined the Federal Theatre Project (FTP), an initiative funded by the Works Project Administration (WPA) of the New Deal. The aim of the FTP, financed by Government money, was to provide work for unemployed actors, producers and writers in the theatre. FTP productions had three aims: to give work to unemployed theatre people and thereby revive the theatre; make the theatre accessible to ordinary people (performances were free); combine a populist, social concern with artistic experiment. Welles, with Robert Houseman, directed a theatre unit of the FTP in New York. Their productions, essentially of classic theatrical works, were spectacular in their settings, costume and stagecraft and in their transpositions of time, in which historical periods were brought together, for example a production of Shakespeare's *Julius Caesar* with actors costumed as Mussolini's Italian fascists or of Shakespeare's *Macbeth* played by an all black cast and set on the island of Haiti. Later, in 1937, because of a scandal caused by a production of the theatrical opera *The Cradle will Rock*, a satire on American political life, the production was blocked by the Government (and with force: police, troops). The company, already known for its unconventional theatre, was disbanded. The incident gave Welles (and Houseman) considerable notoriety.

In Welles's theatre productions two elements are worth remarking on: their insistence on the 'theatrical', 'spectacle', 'special effects', 'magic' and 'make-believe' to startle and attract an audience while making evident the mechanisms that created the effects (nothing was hidden) and at the same time to use the theatre (largely a classical and non-contemporary one in its repertoire) to draw analogies and lessons of a social and political kind. Welles's theatre resonates with the experiments of Bertolt Brecht to make the familiar strange and in doing so involve the audience not only physically and sensually but intellectually, to provoke an understanding and delineate a lesson.

Two realities were made present: that of the theatre and its devices on the one hand and the historical-political reality 'outside' the theatre. Rather than theatre creating an illusion, it revealed illusions. It was less 'like reality' than a dismantling of it. The exterior reality it brought into play shattered fictional conventions of verisimilitude.

Welles's theatre was a play with time, the simultaneous presence, for example in the *Julius Caesar* production of the past (Shakespeare, ancient Rome) side by side with the present (fascist Italy). Times overlapped, were superimposed rather than being linear and consequential. Experiments of this kind that juxtaposed heterogeneous elements from a variety of origins and histories where the real functioned as other, a disruption of a coherent make-believe fictional world, was also a mark of then current American literature in the novel from the relatively conventional (John Dos Passo's *USA*) to the radical and experimental (James Joyce's *Ulysses*); it was also a feature of American poetry (T. S. Eliot, E. E. Cummings, Wallace Stevens), of film (Eisenstein, Vertov) and of theatre (Brecht and Erskine Caldwell).

The best of the film documentary movements in the late 1930s and early 1940s exhibited such a play and negotiation between the real and the staged, for example, in British documentary (John Grierson, Humphrey Jennings), in the photography and films sponsored by the WPA (the work of Pare Lorentz, Dorothea Lange, Paul Strand). These impulses and experiments were evident in some films by John Ford – *The Grapes of Wrath* (1940), *Tobacco Road* (1941) – and by King Vidor – *Our Daily Bread* (1934), *The Citadel* (1938) – and in the first and most famous Welles film of 1941, *Citizen Kane*.

Dramatically (and enduringly) this mix of materials and directions characterised experiments in the fine arts in the 1930s: the Cubist collages of Picasso and Braque, the Dada experiments of Schwitters and Duchamp, the paintings by Salvador Dali and the films he collaborated on with Luis Buñuel.

These elements are equally noticeable not only in Welles's theatre but in his radio productions, famously his adaptation of H. G. Wells's *War of the Worlds*, where the future was in the present, conceived as actuality rather than a narrative of what had already occurred, seeming to be less a fiction than a real happening, an action taking place and broadcast simultaneously as it occurred.

The stake in *Citizen Kane* is the identity of the character (psychological, emotional) Charles Foster Kane, played by Welles, not unlike 'Charlie' played by Chaplin, not entirely fictional but a doubling of a reality. Thompson, the reporter for *News on the March* is sent out in search of the 'true', 'real' Kane by interviewing those who were close to him and who loved or hated him – Thompson's quest is centred on the meaning of Kane's dying word, 'Rosebud', as a possible key to Kane's life and the sense of that life, in short the 'truth'. Kane's identity is constructed by a collage of different narratives and images associated with him. The narratives are fragmentary and contradictory. The more you are told about Kane and the more evidence about him is accumulated, the less you know, essentially because the narratives are from different points of view, overlapping and partial. The film is not one that institutes a subject, but rather disperses and dissipates it in intersecting, juxtaposed fragments, 'views'.

Citizen Kane was made in 1941. From the point of view of the forms and practices of the cinema at the time, the film is a revolution. Most films depend on crucial distinctions between what is (real) and what is not real (imaginary), but in *Kane* such distinctions blur, for example, returning to Chaplin/'Charlie', in the very construction of the character Kane/Welles. It is difficult to know what is true or false, what is subjective or objective, what is real or fake. Every narration by the various characters who remember Kane has strong and different feelings toward him, literally facets, often contradictory. The principal character of *Citizen Kane* is Kane/Welles, the sovereign individual, not only the character, but the act of impersonation. As much as Kane is present, Welles is present. While Thompson is in search of the character Kane, seeking to unify different points of view and stories about him, the unity is never established, not even and especially not even when the 'word' 'Rosebud' finds its 'object' any more than when the name 'Kane' finds its person if for no other reason than that Kane is a fiction of Welles, literally his projection and creation, and that tempts, in the doubling and multiplicity of facets, the desire for an identification.

The real Charles Foster Kane is elusive as are all the characters played by Welles in his other films and most of all in *Mr Arkadin* (1955). The seemingly biographical film of Kane is an anti-biography. It creates its subject not as a unity but as differential perspectives, in effect, a labyrinth. The destruction of unity comes about by a proliferation of words (the narratives, the 'last' word, signs, newspaper articles, newsreels, testaments) and a proliferation of images (photographs, films, memories, flashbacks, clippings, maps, diagrams), most importantly their lack of join and coincidence. Since words and images in the film are out of true and rather than confirming each other tend toward the opposite, words make images doubtful and images make words untrue, or if not untrue, exceedingly ambiguous.

Vertigo ensues of mutual effacements and denials, a centrifuge of dispersals. The search for a resting place, a summary, a coherence, is infinite, above all not only 'Rosebud' and its sled, but between film and audience, the inside of the fiction and the outside of its viewing and its construction (Orson Welles).

Citizen Kane is obsessively concerned with a subject (Charles Foster Kane) and equally concerned with avoiding it. In the end, what remains is not the subject but a void, lured by the false in pursuit of the true. The void and falsity *are* the film and one might go further and say, *is* film. On the one hand, it employs apparently documentary, testimonial evidence (the truth) later exposed as unreliable (prejudicial, lies, fakery, hatreds) while many of the images and sounds (especially voice) are distorted and expressionist as if remembered or as grotesque and parody, not the true, certainly not the 'fictional' true, instead inconsistency and contradiction. The crucial parody in the film is a consequence of the framing of the various portraits of perspectives on Kane that make him grand and larger than life while emptying the image of him of all substance (only words, only images). If the film then destroys its ostensible subject (Kane, the biography), it is also self-destructive, a verbal and visual labyrinth, that separates seemingly connected elements and connects elements that are separated as if working against itself.

Every image in *Kane* is as if cited, an image of an image, including and perhaps above all the image of Kane/Welles, none of which are reliable because the citations are false (fictional, contrived). In the back and forth of the character narratives about Kane absolutely none can be trusted. There is no causation, succession or continuity between them. The narratives overlap or are contradictory. The montage of the film is disjunctive not linear or causative. And most scenes are overblown, exaggerated, excessive either visually and aurally, or at the same time as document and fiction. The famous depth of field in the film, noticed and stressed by Bazin, rather than enhancing reality obscures it by offering multiple planes and perspectives (as with cubism), and using multiplicity to challenge all realistic film representations dependent on coherence, unity and connection. Welles's depth of field is the contrary of the realistic.

It is not that the film, as André Bazin argued, is more realistic because space is not fragmented and left whole by deep focus, but rather is less realistic because what is seen and understood is made doubtful, discursive, open to question and inconclusive, a negation of reality or its questioning as if the film poses to itself, to its characters and to the audience, a permanent uncertainty without any definitive resolution such that any resolution always contains another uncertainty and so on. The more that space is rendered whole, the less real it seems to be because it is internally disunified and incoherent, cut across by conflicting planes, and because it works against the fiction rather than alongside it – the more real it seems, the more strange it becomes, stranger than fiction.

What is radical for the cinema in *Kane* is not simply its infinite gaps and questions, but that even the most elementary aspects of film are put into doubt, become uncertain: voice, performance, time, narrative, space, the shot, the frame, none of which as descriptive terms or procedures really hold.

Citizen Kane narrates not actions, but voices, words, memories, points of view. The voices are different, fragmentary and discontinuous. If it seems that the function of these voices is to provide a unified portrait because of the search for Kane's true identity by the reporter Thompson, the opposite is the case. There is not a single Charles Foster Kane in the film, but multiple Kanes who appear, disappear, dissolve, overlap, contradict, accumulate, superimpose. When the camera glides through the gates to Xanadu and through the sign 'No Trespassing', it enters a world as impenetrable and impermeable as the character of Charles Foster Kane.

Every scene of the film is excessive and distorted and in similar ways. In the narrative in the diary of Thatcher, its first scene is in the modest boarding house of the Kanes, shot in depth where various planes are simultaneously present, from the foreground close-up of Mrs Kane to the stepped mid-ground of Thatcher, then Mr Kane, and finally framed by a window, young Charles Kane outside in the snow. There are many scenes in the film of this kind of vanishing perspectives, overlapping planes, multiple actions, distorted angles and framings, a play with distance through windows, rooms, entrances, exits, corridors, stairs, compressed, made dense, by the low ceilings on the one hand – a lesson apparently learned from John Ford's *Stagecoach* (1939) – and on the other by the grotesque views created by a low-angle camera which press in on the figures as much as do the ceilings. In these scenes sound is superimposed so that voices seem to interrupt or fuse with one another, are warped, hollowed out, given an eerie depth as if issuing from an underworld, like voices from the dead.

One of the problems negotiating the various narratives surrounding Kane is that they lack a centre or become, by their density, opaque, at once too little (inconclusive) and too much (over-determined). The narratives are not transparent in the sense of revealing, as through a window, an irreducible, coherent sight, but each is like a mirror in which every other narrative finds its reflection. Voices and tales told resound, reverberate with other voices, like beams of light that cross and bounce off each another. The effect is literally dazzling, scintillating, sparkling, like fireworks. It is difficult in the circumstances to find your bearings (for Thompson, for the audience), a secure identity or definitive focus. It is like being in a hall of mirrors each reflecting every other, cancelling out origins and identities or, as in the hall of mirrors scene in *Lady from Shanghai* (1947), the target. In losing a secure place and perspective, you lose yourself and in instances in Welles's films, your life.

The play in the film between the search for something definite and its loss and dissolution is partly physical and architectural as well as a narrative effect. There are too many voices, sounds, entrances, exits, distorted angles, clashes, contradictions, exaggerations, too many overlapped planes, too much 'business', too many directions. The effect is overwhelming and dizzying. *Kane* has been labelled 'baroque', presumably for its collision of differences and explosions of space.

There is literally no action in the film, nothing in fact first-hand, except at the opening with the camera entering the magical land of Xanadu and the theatre of the reporters gathered in the studio at the close of *News on the March*, and at the end, a movement not of characters, but of the camera that reveals the identity of 'Rosebud', then departs by the same route by which it had entered Xanadu, through the gates and the 'No Trespassing' sign. Most everything is a double and doubled again because what is told is remembered then depicted second-hand. Essentially, it is a film of second times where virtually nothing is original, pristine or innocent, in that sense, and paradoxically (Rivette's *Jeanne La Pucelle* is a good example), it is a repetition, like history and thereby a loss of innocence (first times).

The action of the film is the words and stories that proliferate, question, deny and contradict. Even when differences seem resolved, to coincide and cohere, for example, at the close of the film, between the sled from childhood and its name 'Rosebud' (*the* search in and of the film, but a search that is a gimmick and pretence like a Hitchcock McGuffin), the result is unsatisfactory, less a resolution than a disappointment. All the spoken narratives literally dissolve into images that are like dreams, encountering not a fullness and substance, but a void, as words and objects pass each other by, uncoordinated, unfixed and discontinuous, like having descended to the Underworld.

Citizen Kane, rather than rendering an image of reality, displaces it with the reality of images. It is a turning point in the cinema from a cinema of action and representation to one of reflection, questioning and discourse. The image no longer belongs to action nor is the setting for it, but belongs to time in which it is caught.

Mr Arkadin

There are three versions of *Mr Arkadin*: the Corinth version, *Confidential Report* and a comprehensive one. *Mr Arkadin* is also a novel, presumably written by Welles, though Welles denied that he was its author. There is, however, no evident other author though there is a French translator, Maurice Bessy. Welles also denied that he ever read the novel. The novel could be a translation from and transformation of the film or vice versa. The first version of the novel was possibly written in French. It was first published in French without an author indicated though the translator, Bessy, is named. It may be that the originally published French version is a translation of an English one or it was the English text that was translated into French then translated back into English, each version of the series being slightly different.

The story of the film is a Wellesian one of deceits, serial versions, the denial of originality and of origins and most of all of a gap between the word (written or spoken) and the image. It is also Wellesian for its play on authenticity and truth and their irresoluteness. Like *Kane*, which was mired in two controversies, one involving the real author of the film, Orson Welles, or his co-scriptwriter Herman Mankiewicz, and the other, concerned with whether the film was a fictionalised account of the life of William Randolph Hearst (Welles said no, Hearst said yes), *Arkadin*, it was claimed, is a fiction of aspects of the life of an infamous arms dealer, Basil Zaharoff, the film as a masquerade, a travesty of an existing reality involving corruption, power, conspicuous wealth and a monstrous personality (themes dear to Welles). These controversies, claims, counter-claims and denials are part of the mechanism of his films and made explicit in *F for Fake* (1974), also a film about authenticity, identity and originality.

It might be said that *Mr Arkadin* is a version of Welles's other films. Many of his characters from these films are ghosts who reappear in *Arkadin*, notably Kane and Welles from *Citizen Kane*, *Macbeth* (1948), *Othello* (1952), *Lady from*

Shanghai as if *Arkadin*, taken as a whole, is a deformed duplicate of the other films and of itself. The elements are similar. The same themes and motifs are present as is the style of distortion and exaggeration of a central figure and of a situation and character magnified to excess, then destroyed. *Arkadin*, like many of the other films by Welles, is constructed by an internal narration – that is, what you see is invented and imagined by the characters within the fiction and thereby becomes doubly fictional, unreliable, misleading, serialised and corrupted, like the glance down a hallway of mirrors creating multiples of the same as occurs in *Citizen Kane*, after Kane's second wife leaves him. If *Arkadin* is a rewriting, a transformation, a doubling or trebling of other Welles films and of a written text whose authorship Welles denies, but which could only be his, they turn the film into a fiction in drag, a travesty, transvestism, self-parody.

Arkadin wears a mask whose purpose is to hide his 'true' identity. But the mask is so evident and so much a charade and lampoon that rather than hiding an identity (identity and its uncovering being the subject of this and other Welles films), it provokes the search for one. By not hiding the act of hiding, it announces, even seeks, what it claims to deny. Welles is scrupulous in denying the truth of any assertion. The relation is complicated. Arkadin is Athabadze wearing a mask. The true nature of Athabadze is to assume the mask, to be Arkadin. And truly being Arkadin is to wear that mask – that is, to be and not to be Athabadze.

Arkadin is the fictional double of Athabadze, in turn the double of actual monsters like Zaharoff (Iago, Quinlan, Kane). Every time the unreality of Arkadin, his mask, is about to be revealed (that he is Athabadze) someone is killed by him to keep the secret while maintaining the idea of it (the truth of it) alive. Arkadin is the idea of Athabadze which when revealed causes the death of both the real Athabadze and his double in masquerade, Arkadin, the true self and the fictional one, the true and the false, both disappearing into nothingness, like Kane's sled and the word 'Rosebud', going up in flames.

The film turns everything into unreality – that is, it invades and demystifies any and every reality which it contaminates, a kind of soiling by exaggeration and disguise. It does so not only by giving reality a mask (distortion), but by pointing to the mask and thereby transforming whatever is into a grotesque other of itself.

Athabadze and his double, Arkadin, is not a singular pair but a serialisation of versions of the same, like Warhol's serialisations. There is no more a unified Athabadze than a unified Charles Foster Kane, or as with Warhol, a unified Marilyn Monroe or Elizabeth Taylor, or for that matter, Andy Warhol. Elusive identities are an effect of plural narratives and plural images, of serialisation that infinitely generate multiple reflections.

Some films (most) create an imaginary world passed off as 'like' reality (a verisimilitude) and so much so that the distance between image and reality is minimised or reduced to nothing (the ideal) as the reality of the image is effaced by what the image represents and thus where there is no 'other' to it internally. Welles instead emphasises the gap and the mask, what hides the truth and the mechanism of the hiding, like a magician revealing his tricks, a permanent otherness and exteriority.

Welles points to the mask by emphasising its contrary and in addition rewriting various versions (the serialisation of characters from one film to another, the similarities between films as if they too are serialised as versions and the fact of identity as the central problem and quest of his films. All of Welles's films make difficult the relation of image to reality, word to image, narrative to story, narration to narrative as with 'Rosebud', 'Athabadze', Clifford Irving's 'hoax', Hank Quinlan's 'confession' caught on tape. What sustains reality and subverts it in *Arkadin* are precisely such gaps. The figure of Athabadze (reality) is sustained by the gap between himself and Arkadin (his fiction in masquerade). Arkadin denies he is Athabadze (the secret), murdering those who affirm the contrary: murder on behalf of a fiction which he protects and which leads to the absurdity of his suicide. The fiction, however, is true. Arkadin is only Athabadze insofar as he is Athabadze's invention, the desire of Athabadze to hide. Reality and true identity are everything that the film is not. The film, like other Welles films, is masquerade, deceit, disguise, posing, ham acting, uncertainty, monstrousness, the grotesque. On the other hand, the process of masquerade, duplication and rewriting is the essence of the film, an essence of pure fabrication by appearances, just as the essence of Athabadze (and his absence, his void) is his appearance in the figure of Arkadin. In both instances a mask is openly assumed and stressed as is the inventiveness and mechanisms of the film.

The central paradox of *Arkadin* and of Welles's other films is that if you kill the fiction (empty it, dislocate it, efface it) you destroy the truth and reality that it sought to belie, but on whose existence it depends as reality depends on fictions in order to exist. The film subsists between these two instances and the convolutions created by their tension. This is the sense too of Welles's *The Immortal Story* (1967).

Welles is no more hidden by his Arkadin mask than Athabadze is hidden by the fiction called Arkadin, but to the contrary the three are revealed by it. Athabadze is the in-between, the fabulous person whose instrument and identity is the fictional Arkadin. Welles's identity is as the person who works to confound identity, covering himself up by wearing a mask (like Athabadze being Arkadin), by making a film in which he is a character whose very existence is its stake, entering into multiple versions of himself and of narratives all of which by being pluralised and with no clear origins are made unstable or disguised. The lure of fiction in the film is not that of a fictional story but of the dismantling of one by the reality that is pointed to outside of it though cannot be possessed by its means, no longer functioning as an illustration of fiction or of reality but of their mutual questioning, tension and exposure.

F for Fake

F for Fake directly cites Welles's radio broadcast *War of the Worlds* (1938) which was based on H. G. Wells's novel of the same name (1898). It also cites the parody '*News on the March*' in *Citizen Kane*, but edited to substitute for Kane-Hearst-Welles Howard Hughes, a millionaire recluse like Kane and Hearst, about whom stories were told and invented, as Welles had invented a story about Hearst, and because it had seemed to be true, suffered accusations of inaccuracies, and enjoyed the diversion of denials, involving libel, deceit and fraudulence that are the subject of *F for Fake* (and of *Othello*): the forged biography by Clifford Irving of Howard Hughes and his possibly equally fraudulent biography of the painter Elmyr de Hory, himself a notorious and successful forger of great paintings and a monumental liar. Welles, like these forgers and like his heroes in his films, has provoked stories about himself and has created himself as a personality larger than life, like Macbeth, Othello, Quinlan, Kane, forgers, illusionists, magicians, liars and mischief-makers all.

There are five principal characters in *F for Fake*: Welles, the Yugoslavian actress Oja Kodar, the art forger Elmyr de Hory, the writer Clifford Irving, and the former art dealer become film-maker François Reichenbach. All the 'characters' play themselves as they are in real life, but in real life their role is not to be who they are: de Hory is a forger, Irving a liar and hoaxster, Welles a magician and maker of films, a pedlar of stories and illusions, Reichenbach a maker of images and pedlar of paintings, and Kodar an actress and seductress (first class), a pedlar of the erotic. None of the characters either in life or in the film that supposedly documents their lives can be believed. *F for Fake* is not a fiction film in any usual sense, nor is it a documentary. It is rather a fiction film masquerading as a documentary. In short, it is fake, like Arkadin, not a fake character (the characters are true) but a fake film where even fakery is fake.

It could be argued, as when Welles, in the last sequence of the film, removes the sheet from Oja Kodar's levitated grandfather, that there is nothing there, that the film is literally empty, an illusion of presences. Rather than a film, there is instead a discourse about it that replaces it. Everything 'in' the film seems to be curiously 'outside' it as if the film lacks interiority, is no more than a location, a locus, a space through which various objects, gestures, stories, persons pass and sometimes intersect, meet or fail to meet. Whatever whoever is – Hory, Kodar, Irving, Reichenbach, Welles, Chartres, Ibiza, Toussaint, Paris – is made to disappear as surely as the little boy's key and the coin that displaces it at the opening of the film at the railway station in Paris, or Oja's sister substituting for Oja, or Oja vanishing into a valise and her grandfather vanishing into thin air (as if he ever was!) while whatever is not is made to appear as if by a series of displacements, erasures, metamorphoses (coin for key, image for object, shadow for person, paintings that are copies or that never were signed by the artists, and artists who didn't paint them). De Hory literally invents Giacometti paintings that were never painted by him as the fictional grandfather invents an entire non-existent Picasso 'period'.

Most of the material in the film was not shot by Welles but by Reichenbach for a film he was making on Elmyr de Hory. Some of the sequences were shot by Welles but most of the film, insofar as it is a Welles film, is a film made at the editing table. If the characters are difficult to identify because they are never true, so too is the film, since it is composed of other films and found footage and because its words (interviews, asides, commentaries – as with *Citizen Kane, The Immortal Story, Lady from Shanghai, Touch of Evil* (1958), *The Magnificent Ambersons* (1942) and, interestingly, *Othello* – are not only the words of unreliable witnesses but issue from places outside the film and its fictional temporality.

The film involves four stories: the story of Elmyr de Hory the art forger, about whose life Irving has written a book (Hory painted post-Impressionist, 'modern' painters such as Matisse, Derain, Soutine, Picasso and Giacometti and so convincingly that he could sell them to galleries and dealers); the story of Clifford Irving who wrote a book that purported to be the official biography of Howard Hughes complete with interviews (the interviews were fake and the autobiographical elements of the book inventions); the story of Oja Kodar's seduction of Picasso enabling her, in return for posing in the nude for the artist, to be presented with 22 Picasso paintings that her grandfather, an art forger, is said to have copied and exhibited as genuine Picassos and then burned the Picasso originals so that only the fakes existed. (Kodar's seduction and story about Picasso is as untrue as Irving's book on Hughes and Hory's paintings while the grandfather probably never existed and is only an actor.)

The material with which the film is composed is various and none of it coheres. It is even difficult to say where the film actually begins. Does it begin at the station? at the moviola? with Elmyr? in Ibiza? in Paris? in Toussaint? with Reichenbach's film? As with D.W. Griffith's *Intolerance* (1916), there is the co-presence of all the elements of film at every point of it, but unlike Griffith's film this co-presence never enters a progressive time; instead there is a constant separation and division of all that might be united and a union of all that is effectively separate: the documentary is not only falsified, but pursues false trails as false and elusive as the identity of Kane, Arkadin, Iago or Welles. Arkadin is who he is not and who he is not is who he is, thus to uncover or discover him, to certify him, is to lose him. His characteristics are elusiveness and deceit, like the character of Kane, hence the emptiness in *Citizen Kane* (and the temptation of fullness) and the lure of the childhood sled that represents nothing and everything. *F for Fake* proclaims it is true but its truth is false, a negative posing as a positive, an identity that is unspeakable, self-negating and impossible to locate.

Lady from Shanghai

As in *F for Fake*, Welles has three positions in *Lady from Shanghai*: he is its author (the film-maker), its principal character (Michael O'Hara) and its narrator (Michael O'Hara), at once in the film (character) and outside it (author), and neither fully inside nor outside (the narrator). Welles is a multitude of images and functions that overlap and issue from different directions. The other characters are similarly multiple as in *F for Fake* and in *Citizen Kane*.

Elsa Bannister is a character played by Rita Hayworth, and Rita Hayworth is a Hollywood image of beauty, eroticism and fatality, a ready-made, a lure and doubly deceitful: she deceives as a character (betraying O'Hara and seducing him like Oja Kodar does Picasso) and she deceives by the fact of being an actress and a star (acting, faking, simulating). Rita Hayworth was then the wife of Orson Welles.

The duplicity and multiplicity of Hayworth-Bannister and Welles-O'Hara are part of the ingredients of the other characters: Arthur Bannister is deceptive, schemes and mystifies. He is grotesque, a distortion, a parody, a reflection-mirage; the same is true of George Grisby and Sidney Broom. In short, every image and every character is deceptive, deformed, divided and split. They proliferate into reflections so severe as to cast doubt on any reality whatsoever (as occurs in *F for Fake* and in *Kane*). The proliferation of figures (and thereby the crisis and instability of identities and of their similitude in images) causes a split to appear between images and what they represent since no image is adequate or conclusive to the reality it supposedly depicts – indeed, the reverse is true: it is the inadequacy, the difference of image to reality that Welles establishes in this and his other films.

The severity of such differences in *Lady from Shanghai* (and *F for Fake*) is directly related to Welles's narrative approach. Welles uses words to question an image, unsettle it with doubt. The words of characters and of the narrator are either confused or deliberately misleading, making ambiguous what it is you see. Rather than words being a support to the image, words are used to undermine the veracity of both: you can't trust words, nor images, nor actions, nor persons in his films especially since points of view (the way you are to look at what you are presented with – that is, the interpretations offered to an audience by a film) are distorted (the low angles, the wide lenses with short focal lengths) and overlapped or sepulchral as are sounds and words, as if everything decomposes and shatters either coming from or dispersing toward an elsewhere. The narrator is neither centre nor guide but a character caught in a labyrinth of words and images mostly of his own making (his story is a story of being trapped, seduced, misled, a story of confusion and inadequacy, of being a victim of himself and of fate), a split where nothing holds together and no path is clear or straight.

The brilliance of the final scene in the Hall of Mirrors in the Crazy House is a culmination of the film and of the manner in which its vertiginous and labyrinthine story is told – the story is a labyrinth as is the telling and weaving of it, a story of split identities, mirrored reflections, impossible mirages that are narrated (by Welles *and* by O'Hara.) The inadequacy of image to reality, words to sense, sound to image, narration to story result in opacity, the decomposition of figures and of time.

Anthony Mann

Anthony Mann made 31 films, his first in 1942, his last in 1964. His films were genre films: *film noir* like *T-Men* (1947) and *Side Street* (1950), super spectacles like *El Cid* (1961) and *The Fall of the Roman Empire* (1964) and Westerns. His Westerns are his most interesting and important films. He made eleven Westerns between 1950 and 1960, five starring James Stewart. *Man of the West*, made in 1958, was his next to last. It starred Gary Cooper, a central figure in Westerns and who grew old with them. Cooper was 57 at the time of *Man of the West*, was suffering from cancer and died three years later.

The Western was the most enduring and constant Hollywood genre. By the end of the 1950s, as the studio system that marked Hollywood went into decline, the Western, along with other Hollywood genres, accompanied it into decline, a decline remarked in Jean-Luc Godard's *Le Mépris*, where forms once dominant become cited fragments. Westerns are infrequent now, but until the early 1960s most directors working in Hollywood had made them.

The Western refers to a time in American history in the second half of the nineteenth century, from roughly the period of the American civil war, 1861–1865, to the turn of the century when the American west had been effectively settled. The Western is the story of that settlement and, insofar as it is, is one of the passing of the west into settlement – that is, the story of its disappearance. It is in that moment between a future that instituted settlement and a past as yet unsettled, of heroes, of individualism and lawlessness, an epic time, that the Western exists. At one extreme is the community in which the hero is no longer necessary, displaced by time and progress, and at the other extreme where the community is not yet, where time, as if frozen, is eternal and repetitive.

There are two dimensions then to the Western. One is historical and nostalgic about the passing of time and the other is epic where time stands still. The Western is the realisation of a history and the struggle against it and, though it records its own passing, the record is equally a record that makes it endure in legend, in film and in popular literature. Film is that history, a tale infinitely repeated of an eternal time no longer.

There is an uncertainty central to the Western in the oscillation between an epic form of repetition and a novelistic one of change and time. The Western hero, certainly in the films of Mann made during a late, last period of the Western, and perhaps its most noble, cannot go back to the past which holds the hero captive nor go forward into the future which impels the hero to advance. And whereas the Ford hero belongs within a community, is its protection and representative and, while not non-violent is not caught up in hatred or revenge, the Mann hero is a loner, often violent and usually filled with hatred.

The Western hero is caught, as is the Western, in a shadowy and funereal world of ghosts from which there is no going back, where only the flotsam and jetsam of the past remain, nor a way forward, where extinction, impotence and cheap vulgarity lie in wait. The setting of the Western is the underworld, the realm of Hades and Orpheus, and one where nobility is present for an instant only.

The adventures of the Western occur in the double time of a fading past and an unwelcome future and involve the essential components of it: individuality and community, wilderness and settlement, eternity and progress, decline and development. Between these, an eternal drama is at stake, a wager with death. You bet your life in the between where for a moment, the moment of the shoot-out, time stands still.

There are occasions in *Man of the West* when Link and Doc Taubin recall the past and when Billie dreams of happiness she never had and will not have in the future except for that precious moment of her encounter with Link. Between instances of loss, memory and nostalgia, of a mutual awareness that there is no going back, except into madness and no going forward except toward vulgarity, the Western lives in the obsessive, risky, actions of Link, Billie and the gambler, to try to survive with dignity and decency where the past and the future encounter each other.

The struggle for survival is a moral one, obeying a code that no longer has a social meaning. The decency of the hero and the fight for life is a fight for the laws of that decency, a loyalty to a code of honour, of being. It depends not on anything written or socially enforced, established or institutionalised but is a manner of behaving, a comportment, courage in the face of time and nothingness. It is to be heroic without the confines or dictates of law and settlement and to have love and dignity outside the social arrangements that accompany them where it is only you and your life that is at stake. Such moments are to be cherished because fragile and their place of survival is in images only.

What is interesting about the moments of dream, intimacy, memory and desire is that they cause a halt to the story, to action and its resolutions and therefore to time. It creates another time, not the time of progress or regression, but a place outside of time, where the story pauses, as during a dance or a song in the Musical. In Ford's films such pauses dominate – the dances in *My Darling Clementine* (1946), *Fort Apache* (1948) and *The Searchers*, the graveyard scenes in *Young Mr Lincoln* (1939), *She Wore a Yellow Ribbon* (1949) – in Mann's film, pauses are few and the movement of the film relentless. The moments of dream and memory and of calm in Ford are modulations and resonances to action, work upon it and modify it. The times of reflection reinstitute time as duration whose only events are events remembered, ones that make of the action that has taken place, is taking place and will take place, also aspects of memory.

Because action in the Western is stylised and conventional, as conventional and stylised as action and descriptions in the epic, ancient Classical ones like the *Iliad* and the *Odyssey*, they too carry on the movement of the film and arrest it, because every action is already a repetition. It is the concrete material of the Western, the actions that define it, and at the same time is an abstraction: the gunfight, fist fight, the saloon, wilderness, lone rider, ambush, Indians. The gunfight in *Man of the West* is crucial to the legends and stories of the West and its frozen, abstracted, perfectly distilled moments. It is in the duration, in the essential emptiness of action, that you feel the reality of time, sentiment and also, I think, the reality of the actor sensing time, aware of it, actor and character going back into the past: the character who is in that past and the actor who accompanies him in a terrible journey forward to extinction.

Gary Cooper's presence as Link and Julie London's presence as Billie give depth to the film. The present that Billie experiences is an experience of the past where the present never existed hence an experience of a future where it cannot exist, and hence the exquisiteness of the moment, of the instant of love and closeness with Link before it too passes into legend and image and unreality, a moment when the film touches reality before it becomes memory.

Man of the West is the story of the violent evacuation of the past by a return to it, repopulating it: the gambler, the dance-hall girl, the ex-killer who literally knock on the door of the past, threatening to revive it, re-enact it as if what the film will re-present is a theatrical tableau, a still life.

All the killers of the Taubin gang are versions of Link in the past, the sons of Doc Taubin, as Link had been his son and no different then as they are now. Each killing accomplished by Link brings him closer to himself. The adventure he has that necessitates a fight for his survival is a survival in which consciousness and action play complementary roles. His survival depends on him returning to that place from which he had escaped in order not simply to put it behind him, but to redeem it, himself and time.

There is power, for example, in the shot that Godard praises in the film, which is the lateral track that takes in Gary Cooper and the town and the dying bandit Cooper has shot. In it, spatial simultaneity is linked with temporal discontinuity since the track begins *after* Gary Cooper moves. The shot exemplifies the dislocation of time central to the film in which Cooper surveys the murder he commits and the ghostly presence of the deserted town of the Old West bypassed by progress.[1] It returns as well to the sequence Godard mentions of the stripping of Julie London by the gang, when, in her underwear, the absent, yet forceful presence of her imagined and desired body, her nakedness, is made apparent. A present image calls up an absent one and it is that absence that adheres in the power of the image. It is the absence of what you see but you are conscious of, the presence therefore of a thought in the gap of its accomplishment just as the Western gives you an image of the passing of the past, of what no longer is at the precise moment when it is present.

Link returns to a legendary past that forces upon him actions to ensure a future where such actions no longer have their place. The future will not possess the virtues that have brought it into existence or the passion and desire that belong to it. The legend is not exactly what was but what is missing from what is, that causes the legend to be told about the passing of time, legend being its own elegy.

What Godard points to in his short essay on Anthony Mann are gaps: a gap in time in the lateral tracking shot and the gap between absence and presence in the stripping of Julie London. In both instances these refer to the larger gap in the Western and in Mann's films of time, action consciousness, the past to the present, the real to the legendary.

The magic of the film is when Link discovers himself in encountering his past as he enters through the door of the cabin where he was young. Cooper is also present, beside Link. The magic is the encounter of the actor with the character, his joining with it, not simply playing the character, but exhibiting the awareness of it, affecting Cooper (an actor in past Westerns) and Link (a character in Westerns), both heroes. It is the moment when the fiction reveals a reality of loss and when reality contributes directly to the force of the fiction attempting to hold on to what is being lost, when for example Billie and Link reflect on the past that comes back and a future that can never be realised and where the faces of the actors and their expressions are superimposed on their characters at an instant when the time of action stands still by the fact of its repetition, its status as legend, the characters as shadows or statues.

The great moments of the Western are constituted by conventional acts, like the gunfight, where the drama of the story is not only played out, but intensified because it abstracts a moment inherent in the drama and because it is also a repetition of an essence of the Western. It is at that moment that story becomes pure style. The transformation of action into style is also characteristic of the American musical, where song and dance take story to a plane of choreography, rhythm, movement, texture.

The modern cinema, especially the cinema of the French Nouvelle Vague, found its inspiration in American films of the 1940s and 1950s, and sought to retell its legends. What was left to tell, however, was only these moments of style, of pure distilled form. *Cinéphilie* is nostalgia and film is nostalgic perhaps, and more so photography seeking to hold fast to what is passing and will be no longer and in that split second when it still is.

Note

1   Godard 1959.

Luchino Visconti

La terra trema

La terra trema was Visconti's second feature film. His first, *Ossessione*, was made in 1942–1943. *La terra trema*, made in 1948, was presented at the Venice Film Festival in the same year and awarded its International Prize, though not the Golden Lion for which it was nominated. Despite such attention, the film was generally not well received and did poorly on release.

The journal *Cinema*

The film journal *Cinema* began publication in 1936. It was one of three film journals supported by the Italian fascist State. The other two were *Bianco e nero* and *Lo schermo*. The editor of *Cinema* was Vittorio Mussolini, the Duce's son. Members of the editorial board included Giuseppe De Santis, Mario Alicata, Gianni Puccini, Pietro Ingrao and Luchino Visconti, all to varying degrees anti-fascists and who, after 1943, joined the Resistance. Some, like Ingrao and Alicata, were important in the clandestine Italian Communist Party. Michelangelo Antonioni also contributed to *Cinema* in which some of his very best film essays appeared. *Bianco e nero* began publication in 1937 as the journal of the newly created national film school, the Centro Sperimentale di Cinematografia (CSC). It was edited by the fascist Luigi

Chiarini and the communist intellectual Umberto Barbaro.

What made this accommodation of ideological opposites possible under Italian fascism was a populism, a going toward the people (propaganda), and the making of 'the people' the centre of representation, hence the essence of what specified the nation, the 'true' Italy. It was in effect realism and nationalism, socially (and vaguely) defined. The line of separation between fascist and anti-fascist was, with regard to the cinema, thin and porous. Besides, populism of the Left or Right assumed the same ill-defined object. Images are ambiguous especially when the stake is 'the real', 'truth' and 'the people'.

The film journals were a response to a felt ideological need by the State to begin to define and shape a national Italian cinema and to help construct by film (and by the media more generally) a suitable image of Italy and Italianness. The journals formed part of a larger investment by the fascist State into film studios (Cinecittà), documentary production (LUCE: L'Unione Cinematografica Educativa), a national film school (CSC), limits on foreign control of the national market (after 1938) and production subsidies to increase and rationalise film production overseen by a newly created (1934) Direzione Generale di Cinematografia under Luigi Freddi, whose models were a mix of the Soviet experience (heroic, ideological) and Hollywood (popular and technically advanced).

Visconti was an active member of *Cinema*. *Ossessione* was both his film and the film of the group. What was remarkable about *Cinema* from its inception, though most evident after 1938, was that every Italian film made was treated in the journal as a national event of cultural, artistic and social-political importance. Films were regarded as crucial for the formation of not only a new Italian cinema but of Italian society and identity. What would become Italian neo-realism critically and in practice was argued out and elaborated in the journal during 1940–1943. *Ossessione* (and *La terra trema*) reflect the debates and ideas in *Cinema* during this period. There was nothing quite like the experience elsewhere except perhaps in the Soviet Union in the 1920s. It only began to be fully expressed in Italy after 1943 with the Resistance and still later with the Liberation in 1945 and by new cultural policies on the Left articulated in the Communist Party weekly *Rinascita*, fostered by the Communist Party leader Palmiro Togliatti, under the influence of a Gramscian stress on the political importance of cultural matters, especially the importance of popular culture, like film.

Essentially, and it is clear in the writings of Giuseppe De Santis and Mario Alicata between 1941 and 1943, *Cinema* was not simply outlining a new cinema, but a new world. Film for the *Cinema* group (and for the State) was *necessarily* political and social in its purposes, hence the emphasis, as a model for *Cinema*, on the social novel of the nineteenth century, primarily French (Flaubert, Stendhal), though not exclusively (Dostoevsky, Dickens), and pre-eminently the narratives of Giovanni Verga, for his populism (the world of ordinary people and their heroism), his settings (the poor, the everyday), his attention to detail ('reality'), his representations of social misery (brought on by fated circumstances), his mix of social document and fiction (the melodrama, close to life but also art), his regionalism and attention to language (the conversion and adaptation of local dialect mimicked in indirect literary speech), and the fact that he was Italian and the aim of the group was to create (invent) an Italian narrative tradition for the cinema, which would become the myth of neo-realism. One of the central strands in *La terra trema* is Verga's *I Malavoglia*, set, like Visconti's film, in the Sicilian fishing village of Aci Trezza.

Neo-realism

Italian neo-realist films, despite their differences (more interesting perhaps than their likenesses), had in common the bringing together of different elements characteristic of Verga's novels: the everyday set within a narrative fiction, a documentary reality reshaped by carefully crafted artifice.

One of the crucial elements in Italian films of the period was their juxtaposition of professional and non-professional actors that contributed, along with the reality/artifice amalgam, to create a situation in the films of closeness (reality, the details of the quotidian, the ordinary and the familiar, real streets, real locations, real countryside) and of distance (form, structure, aesthetic considerations, interpretation, the presence of the author), aspects strikingly evident in Visconti's films from his first to his last.

All Italian neo-realist films (or those named as such) and the criticisms and debates addressed to them centred on how these apparently contradictory dimensions were worked out and related. The differences in emphases between films and directors were defined by the diverse positions taken between the two poles of the aesthetic and the social-political. Visconti's work and notably *La terra trema* strongly evoke these two dimensions and the issues attached to them. They are at the centre of his film and constitute, in their play and tension, its force and interest. They seem, almost, to go beyond themselves as if stretched to excess, as in melodrama. It creates an extremism (the force of a desire that is at once stylistic and social), exaggeration, and thereby, colour, energy and passion, not only in form but in fact (the drama of characters, the drama of a history) that transforms (and juxtaposes) the social and the realistic details of objects, costume and setting into the unreality of myth and melodramatic fantasy, characteristic of Visconti's work in theatre and in lyric opera, both strong presences in *La terra trema*.

Between 1943 and 1948, Visconti staged eleven major theatrical productions and, at the time of *La terra trema*, he staged Shakespeare's *As You Like It* [*Rosalinda*] set in the seventeenth century with costumes and design by Salvador Dali. He was accused by critics (on the Left, in *Rinascita*) of having abandoned neo-realism in *Rosalinda*, by which they meant an absence of social realism. In his defence Visconti spoke of and insisted upon the role of imagination and the possibilities offered in theatre by movement, colour, light, magic, inventiveness, the intersection of times and of styles: '*Non realismo o neorealismo, ma fantasia, libertà totale dello spettacolo*' [*Not realism nor neorealism, but fantasy, the fullest freedom in performance*]. His defense of *Rosalinda* might have also served to describe *La terra trema*, works produced in the same year: the extravagant, Surrealist dandy Salvador Dali placed side by side with the ragged, rude miserable fishermen of Aci Trezza. Which was real? Which fantastic?

The various juxtapositions in *La terra trema* were constructed by Visconti so that each term of the opposition of the real and the fantastic, the political and the aesthetic, gave strength and sustenance to the other, like the 'real' fishermen of Aci Trezza reshaped by him into actors and characters. The effort and training to make Sicilian fishermen, peasant women and wholesalers into actors, into not themselves and yet ..., were exceptional and intense: '*Ho passato ore e ore con i miei pescatori ... per far loro ripetere una piccola battuta*' ['I spent hours with my fishermen ... to get them to repeat a small line']. (Note the stress on '*i miei*' *pescatori*, 'my' fishermen.) The actors are not playing out their lives in *La terra trema* as lived in Aci Trezza, but were characters belonging to another and 'unreal' life in a mythical Aci Trezza, not an analogy – the past/present metaphors familiar in the work of Pasolini, but a substitution.

Visconti invested and integrated the lives of the fishermen into the make-believe of his fiction, using an apparent documentary approach but for purposes opposed to documentary, since the relation of film to the world in *La terra trema* was indirect and highly mediated, a common enough impulse in neo-realist films, notably in early De Sica. Visconti borrowed reality in its minutest details to make a gift of it to art (*i miei pescatori*) and bestowed upon reality the gift of art. It is the artistry, the aestheticising of the real that recalls not De Sica but Gabrielle D'Annunzio and Italian *decadentismo*. De Sica's real seemed spontaneous and therefore close. It lacked Visconti's cultural density and associations and thereby his and our distance, a distance in time and substance. De Sica is sentimental (sickly, thin), appealing to a feeling. Visconti is melodramatic. He displays passion and appeals to ideas.

The beauty and lyricism conferred by Visconti on his fishermen, their boats, their ragged clothes, their humble houses, their slightest gestures give them nobility, make their fate of exploitation and defeat poetic, not simply victims of an economic system, but pre-eminently ancient heroes and warriors belonging to literature, both classical (ancient Greece) and Romantic (the nineteenth-century novel), and to lyric opera (pre-eminently Verga). The characters are the Greeks of Homer and Sophocles, and their language '*è come il greco: non se ne capisce nulla ... una lingua straordinaria, una lingua delle* immagini' ['is like Greek, one does not understand anything ... an extraordinary language, a language of *images*']. And they are also characters from the novelistic of Verga and the film naturalism of Jean Renoir, Julien Duvivier and Marcel Carné extensively written about and praised in *Cinema*. There are traces too of American film noir (melodramas set in everyday realism) and films of social realism, like King Vidor's *The Crowd* (1928) and *Hallelujah* (1929), particularly beloved of the *Cinema* group.

In the film, the Catanese spoken by the characters is incomprehensible except to other villagers. It is less an instrument of communication, certainly not one to the audience, than a sign and spectacle of a hybrid of 'reality' and 'pure' music, the document aestheticised. Such procedures were not those of the neo-realists, not De Sica nor De Santis, certainly not Rossellini.

Time

La terra trema is nearly three hours long. Most of Visconti's films are lengthy, some very much so, such as *Il Gattopardo* (1963) and *Ludwig* (1972). Their length is not, I think, dictated by the needs of an epic narrative and the continuity of events – *Cleopatra* (Joseph L Mankiewicz, 1963), for example, or *The Greatest Story Ever Told* (George Stevens, 1965), or closer to home, Bernardo Bertolucci's *Novecento* (1976). It is rather because Visconti requires time for his images to gather up details, objects and gestures that are themselves products of time, that press together in their concreteness memories, histories, cultures and thereby crystallise and concentrate multiple determinations and directions. Time is required in order to be able to perceive, indeed experience the density. Besides, it is not the narrative that interests Visconti as much as the scene. If it is the case that what is in the space of a scene and delimited by its frame in Visconti exceeds the frame in order to enter time or more exactly in order to allow time to enter (the operatic, for example, specifically Bellini and Verdi; and the literary, specifically Verga; and the melodramatic: Verdi and Verga; in the joyous and exuberant salting of the herrings in *La terra trema*), it is not the case that such movement and association is a dispersion of the elements of the film to an outside. On the contrary, such associations and traces are reinvested back into the frame, back into the images and into the fiction, with the support of time. Time enables the compression, accumulation, maximising. It thickens and textures. For that texturing of overlay to occur, not only is an extended temporality necessary, but so too is distance necessary. Each scene of a Visconti film is stretched out, the camera often travelling through an extended space as in the fight against the wholesalers led by N'Toni in *La terra trema* at the harbour shore in Aci Trezza during the buying and selling of the catch.

Visconti is a film-maker for whom *mise en scène* (a theatrical and operatic practice borrowed by film) is most important, with all it implies for staging, composition in depth, attention to setting and the choreography of movement. It is the space for density, for multiple actions, for resonances between different centres of action and points of association and memories that intersect and in being so, intensified, made passionate. And it is in the scene, held sufficiently long, that objects, sights and sounds are purified into forms contrary to the spontaneity and immediacy that marks neorealist films and that for Rossellini, for example, also entails a paring down and minimising of detail and a disregard for the beautiful, the *belle image*. Beauty is a cultural category. Visconti was centrally concerned with it. To him Beauty was a lost value, one that he sought to recover in his films, and whose cultural disappearance he mourned and also reinstituted, but as a reinstatement that acknowledges the loss, hence the paradoxical aspect of his melodrama, a form from the past that tells a story of the loss of a passion and a culture that it itself exemplifies and presents.

There are two stories in *La terra trema*: the fate of N'Toni and the fate of the melodramatic form of the film. There are no typologies in Visconti, hence it is difficult to specify his politics. N'Toni does not represent a class or a social type in the manner of Eisensteinian typage, the Vakalinchuk in *The Battleship Potemkin*, for example. N'toni may react to a social-historical situation and be the victim of one but he does so as an individual as does Visconti. Neither are examples. It is always the particular that counts. And Visconti's particular is deeply nostalgic and regretful.

Distance and closeness

The opening of *La terra trema* is at dawn, still dark, most everything in shadow except glimmers of light from the windows in the houses of the village, from the streets, and from the lanterns on the fishing boats as they come into the harbour, and the very gradual graying of the sky. What is heard is more important: shouts, cries from the shore to the boats, from boats to the shore, whistles, bells, the opening of doors. The images literally reverberate, not only with elements of a natural music transformed into the operatic, but with time, as if the dawn and return of the boats is an opening into another world, not simply fictional, but ancient and immobile belonging to the past. The use of sound in this opening sequence is similar to the use of sound at the beginning of *Rocco e i suoi fratelli* (1960) as the family comes into Milan station from Calabria and the opening of *Il Gattopardo* (1962) while the family is at prayer in the villa in Sicily. The scene at the harbour sets the stage for the melodramatic challenge to that immobility by N'toni Valastro's revolt against the power of the wholesalers and the tragedy of his attempting it, the desire to institute a change, to break with time and with history, to give birth to something entirely new, more free and open, and the inevitability of defeat, already there in Verga's novel.

Since every character and every act is textured by time and memory, most of it cultural (the opera, the novel, the epic, melodrama, music, Beauty, even Marxism of a Gramscian kind), and however close and realistic, what takes place is narrated over great distances, between historical levels. It is as if one is peering along a vast corridor of time, narrow, dark and enclosed, where each epoch resonates with all others and that, for example, beneath the act of the fishermen returning to shore with the night's catch are other universes and stories within such action, echoing, set into play. Just as what you hear in the opening sequence makes you imagine what you cannot see creates virtual, as yet invisible images, so the Catanese spoken by the characters by its tempo and cadences makes you remember and imagine (and therefore see) all the other worlds to which it is linked and yet belong to worlds no longer there (except as images, as beauty, already the document of something past or passing, and of death). Thus images (and sounds), because invaded by memories, become images necessarily of time, of histories and of loss. They haunt *La terra trema* as they do most other Visconti films, especially his openly historical and political ones like *Senso* (1954), *Il Gattopardo* and *Ludwig*.

Document and fiction

One effect of the introduction into film of a more direct relation between film and the world, whether documentary or not, was to bring into film the aleatory, the immediate, the spontaneous, the unforeseen and unrehearsed, as if it were life itself that had entered the frame, the effect of which was to begin to disrupt established conventions associated with fictional narratives and historical traditions. It seemed to some to offer a new freedom to invent, to express oneself. Part of this opening up of what was conventional was linked to an interest in memory, both as objectively present but also as subjective and historical.

Godard, Resnais and Antonioni, though in different ways – and here, I think, Visconti can enter the picture – pointed out the essential ambiguity and indefiniteness of images, partly because they belonged to histories and memories (and therefore called up associations, of virtual other images and other worlds), and partly because within them were the trace of other images though concretely absent (like memories) and that these absent presences helped to define and shape what was there at the same time threatening all stability. It was also an insight of André Bazin's. No image in this view is singular. All, to the contrary, are plural and multiple by their nature. Rather than trying to arrest this virtuality or define and limit pluralities, Godard (and Godard most of all) encouraged them. At a certain point it seemed only play, as in *À bout de souffle* (1960), but later was more serious and more difficult, for example in *Passion* (1982), because part of the game involved meaning and obscurity and, precisely because it was a creative game that no one wanted to give up, the players were necessarily committed to indefiniteness and even (or especially) obscurity, in order to keep things moving against closing them down in some (impossible, obscene) certainty of messages, of a fixed narrative, thereby ending the game. One result was that film itself became its own subject (an object) rather than a medium to elucidate something else, to illustrate a scene, for example. Film began to approach a modernism already established in the other though not popular arts and particularly in painting, itself undergoing serious reconsideration and reformation in the 1950s and 1960s (POP, Abstract Expressionism, Bacon, the extraordinary work of Robert Rauschenberg).

What was (and is) at stake is the cinema itself, the recognition of an inherent equivocalness and of the gaps and hiatuses in images and between images and between images and sounds and, to go further, that involves the entire institutional and technical framework of making films and projecting them – in effect, the conditions of perception (and production) – and that it was necessary to do battle on behalf of such equivocation and uncertainty and by whatever means. If the document, or the real, or the improvised, or the elliptical and the disconnected were strategies for disrupting a prevailing narrative and fictional verisimilitude, they were equally instruments of disturbance for the documentary conceived and practised as direct social communication, the retailing of social messages to be illustrated and 'served' by the 'medium' of film.

Visconti is troublesome because his path toward preserving and enriching the cinema seemed to have moved in a contrary direction to the one I am describing. Visconti has disrupted nothing. Instead, he has sustained and kept in balance what seems at first sight to be contradictory impulses but are instead fruitful paradoxes. His entire art seems to be founded on forms of the past though not their duplication, rather the sense of their continued value and presence in time and as form – in his case, forms intensely refashioned (as with *Rosalinda*): the purity of sound, rhythm, texture and colour, for example in *La terra trema* within and between languages and by asserting the presence of older literary, theatrical and operatic forms, not exactly as citations, as fragments dislodged from their origins, but rather as recycled material, put to use again, distilled and resublimated. It is precisely by moving away from the fixed and a real to be illustrated, to a real made into form and art, that Visconti's films can be related to other films, take their place in what Godard calls the house of cinema, its histories. The result is not only to set in train the uncertainties of histories, cultures and temporalities present for Visconti in every object, gesture and image of his films, but by doing so to introduce a generalised virtuality, not by an openly declared formalism but by something perhaps more devastating to certified meanings, spectacle and artifice, as spectacles of cultural and temporal layerings and of their passing, of a certain kind of form, then, which can journey, associate, juxtapose, resonate and relate. (It is important to recall that in the 1930s, Visconti worked with Renoir in France.) It is an archaeology of cultural meanings, presented, staged (and incredibly so) by melodrama as if it were lyric opera and the nineteenth-century novel in their ability to combine and integrate heterogeneities of substance, material and form, that performs this task and through (more incredibly still) an emphasis on emotion. Visconti creates out of the past a passionate form to disturb certainties including and perhaps especially, the most 'modernist'.

It was one of the platforms of *Cinema* and of Visconti in the early 1940s to reject *both* an empty formalism *and* a purely objective documentarism in favour of the cultural filters of nineteenth-century fiction, popular melodrama and American film on behalf of a renewal of Italian cinema, of a neo-realism.

The Resistance

The French Resistance in the Second World War was not principally directed to the puppet Government in Vichy of Maréchal Pétain but against the foreign enemy, the German occupiers. In Italy, the Resistance was not only aimed to liberate Italy from the Germans but from the fascist enemy within. The Italian Resistance was an anti-fascist movement and a national struggle and despite its generalised humanism that enabled diverse social groups of different political-ideological persuasions to cooperate, unite and fight together, it was a movement to recreate Italy, to bring it back to life from 20 years of fascism in the hope, especially for intellectuals on the Left, like Visconti and the *Cinema* group, of a popular, democratic, honest and socially just Italy, fundamentally a national rebirth at the heart of which was anti-fascism. If cultural renewal, as a dream, was evidenced in *Cinema* during the last few years of fascism, that hope was strengthened after 1945, after the fall of fascism. Neo-realism in film and literature was the expression of such hope despite the compromises consequent on the vague humanism of Resistance and anti-fascist culture as the price of Popular Front unity. In most every respect, Visconti's cinema, including his early films *Ossessione* and *La terra trema*, is far removed from the realistic and seemingly objective direct relation of film to the world characteristic of the works of Rossellini, De Sica and Zavattini. Nevertheless, he shared the same belief they had that the cinema might make not only a cultural difference in Italy, but a national, political, social and ideological one.

Initially, *La terra trema* was to be a short documentary financed by the Italian Communist Party (PCI) as propaganda in Sicily on behalf of the Party in the upcoming parliamentary elections in 1948. In the event, the Christian Democrats gained the majority with the help of votes from the Italian South and Sicily. The original film was to consist of three thematically and geographically interconnected episodes, one to be centred on sulphur miners, one on the peasantry and one on the fishermen, in each case examples of exploitation attached to the political lesson of the need for popular class solidarity against an unjust social and economic system. Though the title *La terra trema* was retained (the final rising up of the peasantry to shake the earth), only the *episodio del mare* was filmed and not as a documentary, but as a lyrical political-fictional film with documentary elements (as opposed to a documentary with fictional ones). The funds provided by the PCI were insufficient. The film found private finance and Visconti contributed his own money.

La terra trema was to be a political film, a populist going toward the people, in the spirit of seeking, with cultural means (the force of the film) to transform a social situation by the representation and analysis of a social reality (its documentary aspect) to exemplify and dramatise a social truth (by the narrative, by the spectacle, by the beauty and emotionalism of the fiction, by characters with whom you sympathise and who are movingly and tragically defeated). Reality then, but reality mediated, shaped, interpreted, at the other extreme to Rossellini (and Zavattini) where reality filmed is de-dramatised, unanalysed, unfiltered, direct and, most importantly, unresolved and elliptical. With Visconti, who creates melodramas, there is a necessity and inevitability to events. With Rossellini, there is instead surprise, scandal, the miraculous, the unexpected, sudden revelations, as if 'reality' is that something that arrives from nowhere (to disrupt illusions), without preparation, casually and by chance, as in life. In Visconti, nothing is spontaneous or improvised either in his preparation of his films (hours and hours spent on repeating lines, mapping gestures and movements and his concern for the authenticity of the least detail – like a button or what a dresser drawer or a trunk, never to be opened during the film, might contain) or in the final results (the real made into music, rhythm, composition, the aesthetic). Viscontian reality is overwrought, exceedingly construed, and passionately dramatised.

Languages

La terra trema is textured by three languages. The main one is the Catanese dialect of Aci Trezza spoken by the characters. They speak to one another within the fiction. Second, there is the spoken commentary in Italian by Visconti and Antonio Pietrangeli. The commentary is about the characters and their actions. It is outside the fiction. The characters speak in one place and are spoken of from another. Third, there is the text of Verga's *I Malavoglia* whose words and dialogue are worked into the speech of the characters and into the outside commentary (as proverbs, reflections, interpretations; and there is, above all, the Verga story itself, however modified it is by Visconti) as if both characters and narrators are speaking from an elsewhere to which neither belongs. The transfer is more inscription than citation. They issue from different texts and from different temporalities: an archaic, heroic one likened to ancient Greece (Ulysses, the Faraglioni in the bay as the mythical Greek monsters Scylla and Charybdis, the wholesalers' company, one of them with funny eyes, named *Cyclops*) and a literary, nineteenth-century naturalist one derived from Verga. All these are within the fiction, and texture it without causing it to tear. They are the cultural and temporal mediations that give film its resonance.

Citing, as with Godard, is a highlighting, an act of removal and displacement. Godard's citations are the material of his films, one of whose functions is to make it difficult to find a centre in his work since the citations make everything unstable and tend to disperse the film to an outside to a point at which the integrity of both the film (as an object) and what it contains by its forms are placed in crisis. In *La terra trema*, the differences and times, though real, are integrated, fictionalised, transmuted by the film as the Catanese dialect is and as the gestures of the fishermen from Aci Trezza are. Though these are of diverse origins and are layered in the film, they are primarily the material of the narrative, echoes of differences, of pasts into the present that are projected together, calling to one another from far away. It is not, as it is with Godard, a collage of differences but their fictional integration, the means of joining them and including them without homogenising and losing them. Their traces are always evident.

The Catanese of Aci Trezza is a divided language. It is not what the villagers normally speak but rather what they had once spoken and that Visconti caused to be revived. He presented them with a situation that they would improvise into Catanese, which Visconti then reshaped and had them act out and speak, again and again. He worked with the characters for hours, sometimes days on every scene, utterance, gesture and detail that he recast and remoulded to retain in them vestiges (virtual presences) of the archaic and mysterious, a lost past and ancient passions, a speech of rhythms, sounds, tones, inflections not of meaning or communication, or at least not primarily. The film (really a set of theatrical scenes) is organised by Visconti (after

Verdi) into arias, duets, concertante and recitatives, to form a symphonic lyric melodrama, each scene a distillation of emotion, the everyday transformed into the exceptional, the banal into the emotional, the mean made noble and grand, not despite the rags worn by the characters (these are both rags *and* costume, reality *and* artifice), but because of them, and the whole made into music. The more humble, the more intense, the more defeated, the more heroic.

Significance, interpretation and understanding are provided by the Italian commentary. Music, lyricism, unreality are suggested by the Catanese spoken by the characters and by their appearance and choreographed movements. Hence the compounding at the centre of the drama of *La terra trema* of the real and the authentic on the one hand, and the constructed, unreal and aestheticised on the other. The Valastros are not only humble fishermen but are nobles. Their rags are as glorious as the finest robes of kings (the characters are mean and imposing at the same time), not an ordinary tale but an extraordinary one in a mythical land of fairies and giants, larger than life: the giant Cyclops, the monstrous Scylla and Charybdis that wreck and threaten Ulysses. And these larger than life aspects, astonishingly, are, as presented in the film, clothed in the apparel of populism, of 'the people'.

Dreams

In every image in *La terra trema* and in every sound and gesture are engraved other virtual ones of time, memory, history, geography, identities and forms, which is why to give a precise name to these aspects that are so multiple in their directions, cultures and temporalities would deprive them of their richness and power, place a limit on the value of their uncertainties, the range of their intersections and on the fantastic that is called up by means of the concrete realities of the everyday, not exactly the anchors of Visconti's films, but pretexts to be transformed. Visconti takes the fishermen, their families, masons, wholesalers of Aci Trezza as they are and causes them (by an intense artistic effort) to become what they might be or dream of becoming, heroes, even gods. N'toni is his own hero, evident when he returns with the mortgage money from Catania and begins to strut, to plan, to grin, to project, to dance, to sparkle. Such dreams, however they may be cast forward into a future, and made into spectacle, are, like all dreams, memories from a past composed of what is, but intensified into virtualities of what might be, only possible in fictions, but not, as Visconti's films always tragically exhibit, in life. His films are about dreams that never come true, the centre of the melodramatic. And yet, without such realities, without the obstacles, also at the centre of the melodramatic, dreams would be less splendid, less passionate, less filled with desire, would hardly exist. It is their unreality that makes them real, that is, alive, emotional and true.

Performances

There is a double, insistent dimension of Visconti's films, evident I think in the performances of his actors or more precisely in his conception of character. Most of his main characters, certainly the most interesting (and the most doomed and tragic), are dreamers, but they are also, visibly, actors playing a role. The characters are not only played by actors, but are characters who act – that is, perform a fiction, projected to the interior of the film. And it is only by such fictions and the acting out of roles and dreams that they are brought into touch with the realities of circumstances, of history and the social that strip them of their (false) roles and evoke their (true) passions, force them to come face to face not only with the destruction and spectacles of their own making but with the society that caused their dreams to exist at all and stimulated their performances. It is why they elicit our sympathy even though at a distance. The closest film-maker to such a sensibility was Jean Renoir with whom Visconti worked on a film version of Puccini's *Tosca* (1940).

Earlier, in 1934, Visconti had worked on Renoir's *Partie de compagne* based on the Maupassant story and in 1936 on Renoir's *Les Bas-fonds*. Visconti was introduced to Renoir by Coco Chanel. He was put in charge of costuming.

François Truffaut

Tirez sur le pianiste

The script for *Tirez sur le pianiste* (1960), François Truffaut's second feature, was composed each day for the sequences to be shot in response to the rushes of the previous day. It was not as if the film did not have an overall plan – it did – but rather that details were worked out as the film progressed. Often the details were digressions (narratively speaking) or interruptions (of a continuity). The consequences were that the film was perpetually left open and Truffaut could invent as the film went along and as he responded to what had previously been shot and in some cases already edited. The ending of the film was arrived at as the film was being made rather than pre-arranged by a completed script. The film is not a pictorialisation-illustration of a writing, but a 'writing' on its own, closest to the experience of its production rather than to an anterior time of planning.

The film was shot in continuity. What came next was in response to what had come before not necessarily narratively, rather as associations, poetically. This manner of filming gives *Tirez sur le pianiste* a freshness and spontaneity. The film was discovered and unfolded as it was being shot, also made possible because the film lacks a thesis (*film à thèse*) and thus is free to wander and explore sensitive to the moment without the constraints of explicating or abiding by a significance.

Tirez sur le pianiste is a pastiche of different genres and different sources not unlike a collage. It is not that the film lacks continuity or a narrative, but rather that these elements are flexible, attentive, open, changeable and provisional. At any moment, anything can happen, one genre or another can intervene, superimpose itself, altering, even subverting moods and conventions and therefore the film can wander, explore, essay.

Tirez sur le pianiste is adapted from the American *noir* novel of 1956 by David Goodis, *Down There*. The opening of the film belongs to a *film noir* tradition (literary and cinematic) of the 1940s and 1950s, both American and French, by its subject (a figure running down a dimly lit street at night pursued by a car), the lighting creating shadows and flashes between illumination and obscurity. The character in flight is Charlie's brother, Chico. When Chico runs into a lamp post (a comic turn toward the silent cinema), literally creating a new path for the film, a shift from *noir* to comedy, from the present of the cinema to its past, he is helped by a passer-by with whom he has a conversation about marriage (a chance encounter and seemingly an irrelevant one to the 'story', rather like a gag or an unlikely, inexplicable juxtaposition, where the film 'veers' and yet finds another course ... coupling and marriage *is* a theme in *Tirez sur le pianiste*).

The new scene breaks the rhythm of the chase and though a continuity with the previous one, it is also a swerving away. Not only does it vary the atmosphere of violence and dread, the mood that had been established, but also varies its tempo and, importantly, its genre, as the film in this as in other instances passes into a new zone. Such passages, reversals and heterogeneities of elements were characteristic of the *Nouvelle Vague* films of which *Tirez sur le pianiste* is exemplary.

There are many debts being paid, above all to silent comedies and especially to Chaplin. The passage from one realm to another is an echo of Jean Cocteau's *Orphée* where Orpheus passes through a mirror to descend into the Underworld, also the story of Godard's *Alphaville*, itself the story of John Ford's *The Searchers*, where Ethan Edwards (John Wayne) passes into another world to rescue Debbie (a transformed Eurydice?) and all of these instances unmistakably recollections of Ernst Lubitsch's *Ninotchka*, Melvyn Douglas having to descend to the supposed hell of the Soviet Union to bring Ninotchka 'out' for the sake of love (the subject of *Alphaville* and also of *Bande à part*).

Though *Tirez sur le pianiste* goes forward despite shifts, interruptions and disruptions, going forward is less important than movements sideways, diversions, verticals or angles to a horizontal, as if every move is subject to a detour and where the film as purely film intrudes on the film as representation, corroding it from within, creating a double world, double spaces and a doubled temporality that play with and upon one another, not unlike the device of the voice-over in the film where the character comments upon his own thoughts and behaviour, a *noir* cliché that Truffaut manages to freshen.

There is, then, a narrative continuity side by side with discontinuities and seemingly superimposed on each other, alien registers that disturb the fiction as if from some other world beyond it, for example when the gangster's mother grotesquely dies in quite another film in response to words in 'the' film. It is like a gag or like a musical number that 'interrupts' the main story as in the American musical or in a Howard Hawks film and yet belongs to it, carries it on and forward. *Tirez sur le pianiste* has the capacity to sheer off, digress yet sustain the story it dislocates, a change of course, yet one still 'on course', successive and not, sequential and not. Indeed, the digressions depend on the narrative and the narrative on the digressions.

When Chico and his rescuer take their leave from each other at the opening after their conversation concerning marriage (a repetitive motif in the film: the suicide of Charlie's first wife, his love affair with Lena and her death, the strained relation of the café owner and his wife, his temptations to infidelity, and the discussion of women by Fido's kidnappers), Chico enters a café where his brother Charlie works. Charlie is its featured honky-tonk pianist. When Chico arrives, Boby Lapointe, one foot in fiction, another in reality (like Aznavour who plays Charlie), is singing a syncopated word-play song of puns and unlikely juxtapositions whose rhymes take precedence over meaning ('disaster' and 'raspberries' illogically made to come together, as strange a coupling as Charlie and his first wife Theresa, though a more happy one, and rather like – Chaplin again – the Jewish barber impersonating Hynkel in a garbled German in *The Great Dictator*). It is significance 'punned', made rhythmic and melodic, precisely the manner of the working of the film, an incessant out-of-sequence and mismatch. Within the first few minutes of *Tirez sur le pianiste*, there is a movement between genres: from 'the musical' to a 'gangster film', to 'melodrama', to 'comedy', and between words and images. The film is a pastiche, a hodgepodge of forms, directions, tempos and space, sounds and depictions, a criss-crossing of moods and of editing by jumps and collisions rather than by smooth discrete continuities.

Space is not exactly nor simply a matter of a shift between represented locations, from street to interior, interior to street, corridor to alleyway, nor of one time to another without a transition to link them logically, nor even between flat shots that emphasise a surface and those that emphasise a depth, but because of the gap created between different elements, often stressed by the declarative of a jump cut (the violinist walks down a corridor and is then seen walking down a street, a continuous movement in a discontinuous space, space as representational – an image and illusion), and is also concrete, something formal yet palpable, belonging to the gap in disjoins of images, the between of shots and subjects, different times and references, the unrelated integrated and vice versa. The film genres of which the film is composed are less parodied than modified (invigorated, given new life) by associations and by abrupt changes of tone (Fido with the gangsters in the car, the terror of kidnapping in a *noir* movie becoming an absurd comedy of quite another kind of movie). This construction of space is formal and it is to forms and thus to the cinema that *Tirez sur le pianiste* pays homage and to which it is devoted as an act of love.

The narrative of the film is ever present (the film has a story, the story has characters who act and interact, the story can be related, there is a perceptible continuity between sequences and events *and* perceptible discontinuities, jumps, illogic), and the focus of the film is on both its narrative aspects as well as on an elsewhere beyond them, where differences are layered, of genres, of voice-overs (at a different time and space to the action), in cuts (where motive, causation and logic are obscured or subverted and moods shifted), and finally by the presence of the film as purely film in a film (much of which is 'out' of sequence) such that the source of scenes cannot be attributed to a (false) reality that has been concocted *as if* the scenes motivate each other, but because illogical can only be attributed to the activity of the film and its *auteur*, alone capable and privileged to create intransitive transitions and free to do so, to play in the absurd, thus insinuating into the fiction that has the reality of its work, its *mise en scène* as the sign and practice of the liberation of film from a supposed 'realism' and 'representation'. These two 'sides' are present simultaneously.

Just as differences overlap or are interrupted, superimposed, repeated and rhymed, the most crucial difference is between what is presented 'in' the film (by its fiction) and the presenting of that fiction from without it, at the borders between the film as *mise en scène* and the film as representation. Its systematic disturbances in which the space of the film and its temporality are clearly created expose the interior and the fictional as the consequence of what is exterior and 'documentary', leaving behind it less the traces of its characters or their stories than its own instantaneous, sudden and fragile flight, like the tail of a comet, not a continuous linearity, but something unstable (and beautiful – poetic): moments, openings, rhymes, returns, sometimes coalescing like marriage, love, betrayal are in the film, or a coalescence that is purely formal (an idea, even to the arbitrary).

Tirez sur le pianiste is a homage to the American cinema, and I believe also to Charlie Chaplin. 'Charlie' Koller in the Truffaut film is not who he really is even fictionally, but instead a false double to himself, an impersonation. Charlie Koller is also 'Charles' (Aznavour) and someone else entirely (Eduard Saroyan). The real Saroyan (William) was an American writer whose subjects are not unlike Chaplin's: immigrants, the poor, childhood. The *Nouvelle Vague* critics and directors at the Cinémathèque not only celebrated the fictions that the American cinema created (its stories, actions and narratives), but celebrated what made these occur – that is, matters of style – and made of these the subject of their films.

In *Tirez sur le pianiste*, the subject(s) on the one hand, and the manner(s) of representing them, on the other – there are no singularities in the film, no imposed unity – are inextricable and mutually dependent, and even though distinct (the jump cuts, heterogeneity, hodgepodge, disturbance, activities of the camera, of framing, of montage), nevertheless paired, couplets, duets, such that an action or object is itself and an abstract form, a reality and an idea, itself and other to itself, as if every position is only temporary and conditional and moves toward its opposite which is also is a similarity, and, as with Chaplin, a doubling by means of differences and sameness. This mechanism of back and forth, one of instability in *Tirez sur le pianiste*, creates an unceasing, perpetual, imperishable sensation of movement and energy dependent on a wavering between balance and imbalance like Chaplin's gait and the elegance of his iceskating or waiting on tables at once clumsy and graceful, generous and arrogant.

John Ford

She Wore A Yellow Ribbon (1949) is punctuated by dates crossed out in red on the calendar that mark the time left before retirement from the cavalry by Nathan Brittles. It is measured in days and then with the bestowal of the watch by the troop to mark his retirement, by hours and minutes. Brittles does not want to retire, no one wishes him to retire, certainly not the audience, but time and the army require it. The film, like Ford's *They Were Expendable* (1945), brings forward the inevitable and delays it as if waiting for a miracle. And the miracle does come. There is always 'someday', when MacArthur will return to the Phillippines, when America will win the war in the Pacific, when the battle of Midway, despite the losses, will be a victory and when Nathan Brittles, at the last minute, will be appointed an army scout.

And yet there is the melancholy of time passing and its irreversibility. Ford's films are set in the past, are 'historical', and, because we know the present, because we know what will happen since it has already happened, already part of history (the Americans will be defeated in the Phillippines, Custer will lead the cavalry to a massacre, the Old West will die, will, if you like, be retired, the Clantons will be killed at the OK Corral and along with them Doc Holliday, the green of the Valley will become a slag heap), there is the perpetual sense of loss in Ford, of a mournful inevitability, yet the holding back of what will be, a delay, a retardation of time. But it is also, a second time, no longer innocent, a repetition of what already has occurred. Ford's films fall between these contrary movements. It is this between, the holding back that is at the core of Ford's films. He shoots in sequences that alternate between those that move the narrative forward and those that interrupt or deflect it, a pause, without ever losing it. The interruptions, however, those of low comedy, sentimentality, Irishness, dancing, the beauty of a moment snatched from despair, destruction or mourning – Sandy coming to dinner in *They Were Expendable*; Doc Holliday reciting *Hamlet* in a saloon in *My Darling Clementine* (1946); Olivia's shadow falling on the gravestone of Nathan Brittle's wife in *She Wore a Yellow Ribbon*; Lincoln placing the first snowdrops of Spring on the grave of Annie Rutledge in *Young Mr Lincoln* (1939); Martha caressing Ethan's coat in *The Searchers* (1956); Sean Thornton's first sight of Mary Kate Danaher in *The Quiet Man* (1952) – not only delay the inevitable but are the reasons for the delay. It is why time is deferred, to make what is passing precious and to hold on to it for an eternal instant. The sense that nothing will last makes it precious and yet because it is precious it seems imperishable.

There are two perfections in Ford's films. One is compositional and essentially visual, the way movements are choreographed in the frame whether it be of riders strung out across a rise, shadows disappearing into the dust or into darkness, the grouping of cavalry, the organisation of a party, a ball, a dinner, a fight, sailors (or boats) peeling off from a dock individually or in small groups, orchestrated 'at ease', an Indian attack, a lynch mob. The appreciation of these moments is not exactly after they occur in which you can say, or the film says, 'look, isn't this beautiful', but rather it seems to be anticipated as if coming before itself and it does so because it belongs to the past. Even the most violent scenes, or the most silly, are elegiac. And because what you see is so wonderfully organised and since you will never see it again, it is at once instantaneous and contemplative, perfect harmony and balance, not to be upset or dismantled, but only to disappear – a disappearance, however, that is merely historical, the image of it will remain.

The other is rhythmic and essentially musical. Part of it is the moving forward of the narrative and the delays that temporarily halt it like interludes or elaborations of a minor key or tone brought gracefully (Ford is never jarring) into prominence and the counterpointing of dominant and minor, neither of which is ever sustained, because nothing in Ford is ever finished, nothing concluded since the past is never gone because the film endures. His films are the tombstones of that presence addressed by Ford as Nathan Brittles, Lincoln, Judge Priest and Hallie Stoddard address the dead whom they still love and so intensely as to make them live, like a photograph of an instant to be contemplated indefinitely.

Because Ford's films are set in the past, everything you see is a second time, a double of what was, as with all representations, yet Ford manages to make the second time seem first, as if it is not exactly the past brought back and made alive, nor a return, nor reinstatement, but the original and by that fact preserves its innocence that perhaps accounts for the thrill and palpitation when the credits come up in a Ford film. He seems able to make true and present, what can never be so, without asserting the one or denying the other, hence the elegiac melancholy and lyricism of his films.

Bibliography

Abel, Richard (1984), *French Cinema: The First Wave, 1915–1929*. Princeton, NJ: Princeton University Press.

Amengual, Barthélemy (1997), 'Jean-Luc Godard et la remise en cause de notre civilisation de l'image', in *Du Réalisme au cinéma*. Paris: Nathan.

—— (1997), 'L'étrange comique de Monsieur Tati', in *Du Réalisme au cinéma*. Paris: Nathan.

—— (1997), 'Monde et vision du monde dans l'oeuvre de Vigo', in *Du Réalisme au cinéma*. Paris: Nathan.

Anderson, Lindsay (1981), *About John Ford*. New York: McGraw Hill.

Andrew, Dudley (1995), *Mists of Regret*. Princeton, NJ: Princeton University Press.

Antonioni, Michelangelo (1949), '*La terra trema*'. *Bianco e nero* 7 (July).

Aragon, Louis (1965), 'Qu'est-ce que l'art Jean-Luc Godard'. *Lettres françaises* 1103 (October).

Aumont, Jacques (1999), *Amnésies: Fictions du cinéma d'après Jean-Luc Godard*. Paris: P.O.L.

—— (2002), *Les théories des cinéastes*. Paris: Nathan.

——, Jean-Louis Comolli, Jean Narboni and Sylvie Pierre (1968), 'Entretien avec Jacques Rivette: Le temps déborde'. *Cahiers du cinéma* 204 (September); also in Antoine de Baecque (ed.) (1999), *La Nouvelle Vague*. Paris: Cahiers du cinéma.

Badiou. Alain (1998), 'Le plus de voir' in 'Guide pour *Histoire(s) du cinéma*'. *Cahiers du cinéma* (November), Paris: Art Press (hors série).

Baldelli, Pio (1973), *Luchino Visconti*. Milan: Gabrielle Mazzotta.

Bazin, André (1947), 'Beauté du hasard: Le film scientifique', in *Le cinéma français de la Libération à la Nouvelle Vague (1945–1958)* (1998). Paris: Cahiers du cinéma.

—— (1954), 'Hitchcock contre Hitchcock'. *Cahiers du cinéma* 39 (October).

—— (1994), 'La Terre tremble'. *Qu'est-ce que le cinéma?* Paris: Éditions du Cerf; orig. published in *Esprit*, December 1948.

——(1994), 'M. Hulot et le temps', in *Qu'est-ce que le cinéma?* Paris: Éditions du Cerf.

—— (2007), *Orson Welles*. Paris: Cahiers du cinéma.

—— and François Truffaut (1958), 'Entretien avec Jacques Tati'. *Cahiers du cinéma* 14(83) (May).

Bellavita, Andrea (2006), *Luchino Visconti: il teatro dell'immagine*. Rome: Ente dello Spettacolo.

Bellos, David (1999), *Jacques Tati*. London: Harvill Press.

Bellour, Raymond (1993), 'MANN (Anthony), in Raymond Bellour (ed.), *Le Western*. Paris: Gallimard.

—— and Mary Lee Bandy (1992), *Jean-Luc Godard: Son + Image*. New York: Museum of Modern Art.

Benoliel, Bernard (2004), *L'Homme de la plaine*. Paris: Cahiers du cinéma.

Bergala, Alain (1982), 'Rivette, Baptiste et Marie'. *Cahiers du cinéma* 333 (March); also in Antoine de Baecque (ed.) (2001), *Vive le cinéma français!* Paris: Cahiers du cinéma.

—— (ed.) (1985), *Jean-Luc Godard par Jean-Luc Godard*. Paris: Cahiers du cinéma.

—— (1999), *Nul mieux que Godard*. Paris: Cahiers du cinéma.

Bernardi, Sandro (2000), '*La terra trema*: Il Mito, Il Teatro, la Storia', in Veronica Pravadelli, *Il cinema di Luchino Visconti*. Venice: Marsilio.

Bitsch, Charles and Claude Chabrol (1957), 'Entretien avec Anthony Mann'. *Cahiers du cinéma* 69 (March).

Bonitzer, Pascal (1981), 'It's Only a Film/où La Face du Néant'. *Framework* 14.

Borges, Jorge Luis (1945), 'Citizen Kane'. *Sur* 83.
Bourgeois, Nathalie, Bernard Benoliel, and Stéfani de Loppinot (eds) (2000), *Atalante: Un film de Jean Vigo*. Paris: Cinémathèque Française.
Brenez, Nicole, David Faroult, Michael Temple, James Williams and Michael Witt (eds) (2006), *Jean-Luc Godard: Documents*. Paris: Centre Pompidou.
Cahiers du cinéma (ed.) (1990), 'Numéro spécial Godard'. *Cahiers du cinéma* (November).
—— (ed.) (1998), 'Guide pour *Histoire(s) du cinéma*'. *Cahiers du cinéma*, hors-série (November).
—— (ed.) (2007), '*Histoire(s) du cinéma*'. *Cahiers du cinéma* 625 (July/August).
Callahan, Vicki (2005), *Zones of Anxiety*. Detroit, MI: Wayne State University Press.
Cerisuelo, Mark (1989), *Jean-Luc Godard*. Paris: Lherminier.
Chabrol, Claude and François Truffaut, 'Entretien avec Alfred Hitchcock' [1955] suivi d'un 'Nouvel entretien' by Jean Domarchi and Jean Douchet [1959], in Daney 2001.
Chateau, Dominique, A. Gardies and F. Jost (eds) (1981), 'Cinéma de la modernité: films, théories' (Colloque à Cerisy). Paris: Klincksieck.
Chion, Michel (1987), *Jacques Tati*. Paris: Cahiers du cinéma.
—— (1998), *Le Son*. Paris: Nathan.
Collet, Jean (2004), *John Ford: La violence et la loi*. Paris: Éditions Michalon.
Daney, Serge (1988), 'John Ford for ever'. *Libération* 18 (November).
—— (1996), 'Éloge de Tati', in *La rampe*. Paris: Cahiers du cinéma.
—— (1998), '"L'amour par terre". *Ciné journal* Vol. II/1983–1986'. Paris: Cahiers du cinéma.
—— (1998), *Vertigo. Ciné journal* II (1983–1986). Paris: Cahiers du cinéma.
—— (ed.) (2001), *La Politique des auteurs: Les entretiens*. Paris: Cahiers du cinéma.
de Baecque, Antoine (2000), 'Quel cinéma après Auschwitz?' *Cahiers du cinéma*, hors-série (November).

——, Antoine (2003), *La Cinéphilie: Invention d'un regard, histoire d'une culture 1944–1948*. Paris: Fayard.
——, Antoine (2010), *Godard: biographie* Paris: Bernard Grasset.
—— and Serge Toubiana (2001), *François Truffaut*. Paris: Gallimard.
Deleuze, Gilles (1976), 'Six fois deux: Sur et sous la communication'. *Cahiers du cinéma* 271 (November).
—— (1986), *Cinema 1*. Minneapolis: University of Minnesota Press.
—— (1989), *Cinema 2*. Minneapolis: University of Minnesota Press.
Depardon, Raymond (2000), *Errance*. Paris: Éditions du Seuil.
—— (2006), *La ferme du Garet*. Paris: Actes Sud.
—— (2008), *La terre des paysans*. Paris: Éditions du Seuil.
—— (2010), *Afrique(s)*. Paris: Editions Point.
—— and Alain Bergala (2006), *New York*. Paris: Cahiers du Cinéma.
—— and Frédéric Sabouraud (1993), *Depardon/Cinéma*. Paris: Cahiers du cinéma.
Didi-Huberman, Georges (2003), *Images malgré tout*. Paris: Éditions de Minuit.
Doniol-Valcroze, Jacques (1958), 'Tati sur les pattes de l'oiseau'. *Cahiers du cinéma* 14(82) (April).
Douchet, Jean (1999), *Hitchcock*. Paris: Cahiers du cinéma.
Eisenstein, Sergei (1970), 'Mr Lincoln by Mr Ford'. *Film essays and a Lecture*. New York: Praeger.
Esquenazi, Jean-Pierre (2001), *Hitchcock et l'aventure de Vertigo*. Paris: CNRS Éditions.
Farassino, Alberto (1999), '*Histoire(s) du cinéma*. Il libro'. *Bianco e nero* 3–4 (May–August).
—— (2004), *Scritti strabici*. Milan: Baldini, Castoldi, Dalai, pp. 96–7.
Faure, Élie (1934), 'Un cinéaste-né: Jean Vigo, auteur de *l'Atalante*'. *Pour Vous* 31 (mai).
Fieschi, Jean-André and André-S Labarthe (1963), 'Nouvel entretien avec Georges Franju'. *Cahiers du cinéma* 149 (November).

Frappat, Hélène (2001), *Jacques Rivette, Secret compris*. Paris: Cahiers du cinéma.
Frodon, Jean-Michel (2005), 'Vous me filmez? Pour quoi faire?' *Cahiers du cinéma* 598 (February).
—— (2008), 'Entretien avec Raymond Depardon et Claudine Nougaret'. *Cahiers du cinéma* 638 (October).
Furet, François (2000), 'Lettre(s) à Godard'. *Cahiers du cinéma*, hors-série (November).
Gallagher, Tag (1986), *John Ford*. Berkeley, CA: University of California Press.
Gauthier, Patrice and Francis Lacassin (2006), *Louis Feuillade: Maître du cinéma populaire*. Paris: Gallimard.
Godard, Jean-Luc (1959), 'Super Mann'. *Cahiers du cinéma* 92 (February).
—— (1980), *Introduction à une véritable histoire du cinéma*. Paris: Editions Albatros.
—— (1996), 'À propos de cinéma et d'histoire'. *Trafic* 18 (Spring).
—— and Youssef Ishaghpour (2000), *Archéologie du cinéma et mémoire du siècle*. Tours: Farrago.
Gottlieb, Stanley (ed.) (1995), *Hitchcock on Hitchcock*. London: Faber & Faber.
Goudet, Stéphane (2002), *Jacques Tati*. Paris: Cahiers du cinéma.
Hamery, Roxane (2008), *Jean Painlevé: le cinéma au coeur de la vie*. Renne: Presses Universitaires de Rennes.
Ishaghpour, Youssef (2001), *Orson Welles cinéaste: Une caméra visible*, 3 vols. Paris: Éditions de la Différence. Vol. I, pp. 227–8, Vol. II, pp. 333–6.
Lagny, Michèle (2002), *Luchino Visconti*. Paris: BIFI.
Liandrat-Guigues, Suzanne (1999), *Le couchant et l'aurore: Sur le cinéma de Luchino Visconti*. Paris: Méridiens Klincksieck.
MacCabe, Colin (2003), *Godard*. London: Bloomsbury.
Martini, Andrea (ed.) (1999), *Georges Franju*. Santa Maria degli Angeli: Il Castoro.
Meranger, Thierry (2008), 'Paysans et modèles'. *Cahiers du cinéma* 638 (October).

Mereghetti, Paolo (1998), *Orson Welles*. Paris: Cahiers du cinéma.
Miccichè, Lino (ed.) (1994), *La terra trema: Analisi di un capolavoro*. Turin: Centro Sperimentale di Cinematografia.
Mitry, Jean (1954), *John Ford*. Paris: Éditions Universitaires.
—— (1980), 'Jean Vigo', in Jean Mitry *Histoire du cinéma: Art et Industrie*, Vol. 4, *Les années 30*. Paris: Jean-Pierre Delarge, pp. 330–7.
Narboni, Jean (ed.) (1980), *Alfred Hitchcock*. Paris: Éditions de L'Étoile/Cahiers du cinéma.
Nel, Noël (2001), 'Histoire(s) du cinéma 1 et 2 de Godard', in Gilles Delavaud, Jean-Pierre Esquenazi and Marie-Françoise Grange, *Godard et le métier d'artiste*. Paris: L'Harmattan.
Neyrat, Cyril (2006), 'Un vieil endroit'. *Cahiers du cinéma* 611 (April).
Nowell-Smith, Geoffrey (1967), *Visconti*. London: Doubleday.
Paini, Dominique (ed.) (1998), 'Guide pour *Histoire(s) du cinéma*'. *Cahiers du cinéma*, hors-série (November).
Parigi, Stefania (1994), 'Il dualismo linguistico', in Lino Miccichè (ed.), *La terra trema: Analisi di un capolavoro*. Turin: Centro Sperimentale di Cinematografia.
—— (2009), *Cinema-Italy*. Manchester: Manchester University Press.
Rancière, Jacques (2000), 'Le cinéma dans la "fin" de l'art'. *Cahiers du cinéma* 552 (December).
—— (2001), 'Une fable sans morale: Godard, le cinéma, les histoires', in *La Fable cinématographique*. Paris: Editions du Seuil.
Rieupeyrout, Jean-Louis (1964), 'Anthony Mann ou le western exemplaire', in *La Grande aventure du western*. Paris: Éditions du Cerf.
—— (1964), *La Grande aventure du western*. Paris: Éditions du Cerf.
Rivette, Jacques (1985), 'The Age of *metteurs en scène*', in Jim Hillier (ed.), *The Cahiers du Cinéma: the 1950s: Neo-Realism, Hollywood, New Wave*. Cambridge, MA: Harvard

University Press; originally 1954, 'L'Age des metteurs en scène'. *Cahiers du cinéma* 31 (January).

Rohmer, Eric (1989), 'Alfred Hitchcock's *Vertigo*', in *The Taste for Beauty*. Cambridge: Cambridge University Press, originally published 1959 as 'L'Hélice et l'idée'. *Cahiers du cinéma* 93 (March).

—— and Claude Chabrol (2006), *Hitchcock*. Paris: Ramsay Poche Cinéma.

Rollet, Patrice and Nicolas Saada (eds) (1990), *John Ford*. Paris: Editions de l'Étoile/Cahiers du cinéma.

Rosen, Miriam (2001), 'Direct to Film – Interview with artist Raymond Depardon'. *Artforum* (February).

Rosenbaum, Jonathan (2007), *Discovering Orson Welles*. Berkeley, CA: University of California Press.

Sadoul, Georges (1951), *Histoire générale du cinéma 3. Le cinéma devient un art 1909–1920*. Paris: Denoël.

Sartres, Jean-Paul (1945), 'Quand Hollywood veut faire penser ... *Citizen Kane*, film d'Orson Welles'. *L'Écran français* 5 (August).

Scemana, Céline (2006), *Histoire(s) du cinéma de Jean-Luc Godard: La force faible d'un art*. Paris: L'Harmattan.

Schifano, Laurence (1990), *Luchino Visconti*. London: Collins.

—— (1999), '*Histoire(s) du cinéma*: Il capitolo italiano'. *Bianco e nero* 3–4 (May–August).

Silverman, Kaja and Harun Farocki (1998), *Speaking about Godard*. New York: New York University Press.

Somigli, Luca and Mario Moroni (eds) (2004), *Italian Modernism*. Toronto: University of Toronto Press.

Tavernier, Bertrand (2008), *Amis Américains*. Lyons: Institut Lumière/Actes Sud.

Temple, Michael (2005), *Jean Vigo*. Manchester: Manchester University Press.

Tesson, Charles (2000), 'Entretien avec Jean-Luc Godard: Avenir(s) du cinéma'. *Cahiers du cinéma*, hors-série (April).

Toubiana, Serge (2008), 'Depardon (Image) + Nougaret (Son) = La Vie Moderne'. *Blog Cinémathèque/fr* 2 (November).

Truffaut, François (1953), 'En avoir plein la lune'. *Cahiers du cinéma* 25 (July).

—— (1959), 'Entretien avec Georges Franju'. *Cahiers du cinéma* 101 (novembre).

—— (1974), 'God Bless John Ford', in *The Films in My Life*. New York: Da Capo Press.

—— (1994), *Mon Oncle (1958) The Films in My Life*. New York: Da Capo Press.

Vigo, Luce (2002), *Jean Vigo*. Paris: Cahiers du cinéma.

Zagury, Fabrice (1998), *'The Public is My Master': Louis Feuillade and* Les Vampires. Film Preservation Associates.

EU authorised representative for GPSR:
Easy Access System Europe, Mustamäe tee 50,
10621 Tallinn, Estonia
gpsr.requests@easproject.com